Praise for *Reflections of Alan Turing*

'Fascinating and highly readable ... My wife Rohini and I feel particularly grateful to have a special link to [Alan Turing] through our house in Coonoor ... where Alan's mother lived for many years'

Nandan Nilekani, Chairman and
Co-Founder of Infosys

'Essential reading for anyone who thinks they know the history of Alan Turing ... a significant reappraisal of his meaning for us today'

Dr Tilly Blyth, Head of Collections,
Science Museum

'Dermot compels us to learn from his uncle's incredible life and many achievements in our own pursuit of creating a better world for all'

Liz Carr, Actress and Comedian

T0043090

About the Author

Dermot Turing spent his career in the legal profession before turning to writing. His biography of his uncle, *Alan Turing Decoded*, is widely acclaimed, and his book *X, Y and Z: The Real Story of How Enigma Was Broken* won the Polish 'Guardian of Memory' prize in 2019. His other books include *The Codebreakers of Bletchley Park* and *The Story of Computing*.

In addition to writing, he is a trustee of The Turing Trust, a charity which refurbishes old computers in order to equip schools in Africa, and keeps up his interest in the legal issues relating to financial market infrastructures. He is a visiting fellow at Kellogg College, Oxford.

www.dermotturing.com

REFLECTIONS OF ALAN TURING

A RELATIVE STORY

First published 2021
This paperback edition first published 2022

The History Press
97 St George's Place, Cheltenham,
Gloucestershire, GL50 3QB
www.thehistorypress.co.uk

British Library Cataloguing in Publication Data.
A catalogue record for this book is available from the British Library.

ISBN 978 1 80399 012 5

Typesetting and origination by The History Press
Printed and bound in Great Britain by TJ Books Limited, Padstow, Cornwall.

Trees for LYfe

CONTENTS

ACKNOWLEDGEMENTS

In some ways, this is an unconventional book, and bringing it to life would not have been possible without the support and contributions of many people.

Foremost, I must thank Laura Perehinec of The History Press and Katie Read of Read Media for nurturing the idea from the beginning and helping shape it. Inspiration has come from many sources: the blog of Margaret Makepeace at the British Library pointed me to the story of John William Turing; Edith and Florence Stoney now have their own biography by Adrian Thomas and Francis Duck, from which I learned a great deal; Professor Juliet Floyd's writings on Alan Turing in connection with philosophy have deepened my understanding of his work; and Dr James Peters gave me access to the new Alan Turing archive at Manchester University, which I have drawn on extensively to interpret Alan's final years and his relationships with colleagues and correspondents. Also in Manchester, the discoverer of the new Turing papers Professor Jim Miles not only gave his encouragement but also told me about Alan Turing's calculating machine. In Cambridge, and notwithstanding the problems of lockdown,

Dr Patricia McGuire arranged the spectroscopic imaging of correspondence redacted by my grandmother so we could try to find out what she wanted to hide; I am in debt to the Provost and Scholars of King's College, Cambridge, and to Maciej Pawlikowski for making that possible.

In the United States, I was able to find out about the secret Army Bombe project with the help of Dr Philip Marks and the ever-helpful staff of the National Archives Records Administration. The cover image of Alan Turing is also an American creation: commissioned by Princeton University and painted by Jordan Sokol, it is a stunning addition to the iconography and I am grateful to them both for allowing it to be used here. A different approach to art is taken by Justin Eagleton whose quirky and imaginative images allow us to look at Alan Turing in new ways: thanks to him as well for being involved in the project. Others whose various contributions have guided me along the way include Rachel Hassall, Andrew Hodges, Serena Kern-Libera, Kriti Majan, Jezz Palmer, Jonathan Swinton and Colin Williams: thank you to you all.

A special thank you is due to Kayisha Payne for being involved in the project and for all the work she is doing to advance the prospects of young black people in science, technology, engineering and mathematics.

Quotations from Alan Turing's letters, located in the archives at King's College, Cambridge and the University of Manchester, are made possible with the kind permission of the Provost and Scholars of King's College, Cambridge. Quotations from Beatrice Worsley's letters in the Manchester archive are made with kind permission of Alva Worsley.

FAMILY TREES

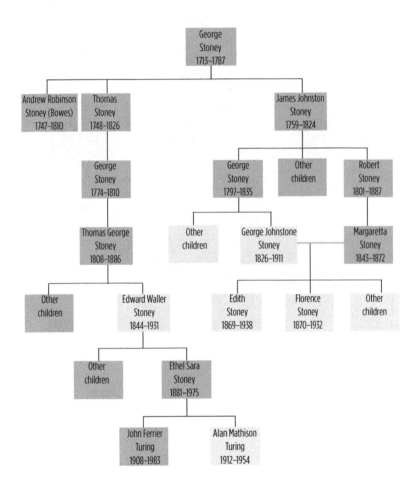

George
Stoney
1713–1787

Andrew Robinson
Stoney (Bowes)
1747–1810

Thomas
Stoney
1748–1826

James Johnston
Stoney
1759–1824

George
Stoney
1774–1810

George
Stoney
1797–1835

Other
children

Robert
Stoney
1801–1887

Thomas George
Stoney
1808–1886

Other
children

George Johnstone
Stoney
1826–1911

Margaretta
Stoney
1843–1872

Other
children

Edward Waller
Stoney
1844–1931

Edith
Stoney
1869–1938

Florence
Stoney
1870–1932

Other
children

Other
children

Ethel Sara
Stoney
1881–1975

John Ferrier
Turing
1908–1983

Alan Mathison
Turing
1912–1954

Stoneys
with science
qualifications

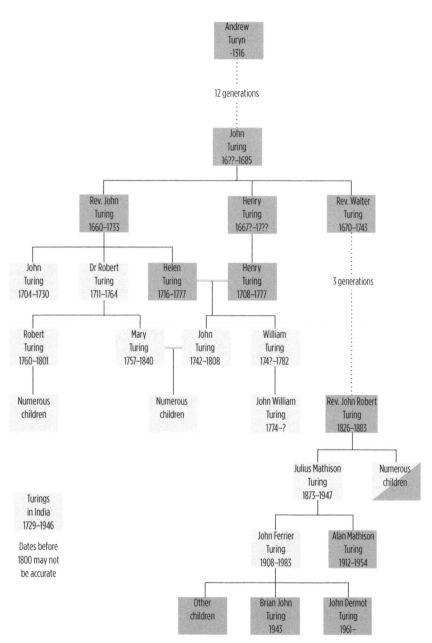

FOREWORD
BY KAYISHA PAYNE

As a young Black woman studying for a master's degree in Chemical Engineering at university, I knew what it was to feel different. I was amongst a minority of woman on the course and an even smaller minority being Black. This was the year 2017 – around sixty-three years after Alan Turing lived and worked – yet many aspects of his story resonate with my experience.

Alan was most famously known for his intellect but, as with every person, there is so much more beneath the surface. The complexities of our lives are often hidden behind our achievements and successes but are equally as important; they are the context of our story. This book unearths many aspects and influences in Alan's life; the one which resonates most with me is his experience of race, which is the basis of my non-profit-organisation, BBSTEM – Black British Professionals in STEM.

The idea for BBSTEM came about whilst I was still studying. By chance I was introduced to a Black British chemical engineer and, as we spoke, I was inspired by him and the story of his career journey. I had never met another Black person in the same field as me. Afterwards I reflected on this meeting and how much value could be gleaned from a meeting that happened accidentally; imagine what could be achieved if a specific community was created with a purpose to help Black people see themselves in scientific and engineering roles as a career, and have a forum where they could ask questions without any judgement? I founded BBSTEM with the aim to encourage, enable and energise individuals in business, industry and education to widen participation and contribution of Black individuals in the field of Science, Technology, Engineering and Mathematics (STEM). A big part of our work is to inspire young Black people to get involved in these subjects at school and beyond, and to show the younger generation that a successful and exciting career in STEM is achievable.

Though Alan Turing may not have faced the same obstacles as the young people we work with at BBSTEM, the message still resonates: we can overcome life's challenges and reach our goals through hard work and resolve. Our life circumstances do not have to limit us. There are also lessons we can learn from his legacy about persistence, determination and being true to yourself. Just because someone says you're wrong or you can't do it doesn't make it so; indeed, like him, you could prove people wrong and go on to become a British icon!

Unlike when Alan was alive, STEM subjects are no longer mainly theory or science fiction. The possibilities to discover and create are infinite. It's an exciting time to get involved in STEM, for old and young people alike. 'Geeky' is no longer a negative. In an age of portable and wearable technology, the people who know how it works and how to create it are the new heroes. And the opportunities to rise to the top, if that's where you want to go, are becoming more open to everyone, regardless of background, gender, sexuality, ethnicity or anything else.

This book needed to be written. It is a story of inspiration; of the struggles of life; of resilience; of achievement; and, perhaps most importantly, of legacy. We all deserve to leave a legacy which is fair and true. Dermot, Alan's nephew, eloquently reveals the puzzle pieces of Alan Turing that the world has never been privy to and allows readers to see the full picture of this man's extraordinary life. All of us have something to learn from him.

As we enter a year in which the United Kingdom is celebrating Alan Turing's contribution by making him the face of the new £50 note, let's reflect on the building blocks that make up the story of our own lives and how they make us who we are. Let's celebrate ourselves, our community and our diversity. Let's focus on the future.

Kayisha Catherine Ibijoki Payne
December 2020

REFLECTIONS

We all own a bit of Alan Turing now. He has become an icon, a symbol, a personification of ideals which he never was in his lifetime, a public screen onto which we can project our own image of what we would like him to stand for, something of which to be proud. His work and life story have inspired the creation of plays, statues, songs, feature films, poems, sound-and-light displays, and even scientific conferences. Many of these are the offspring of a standard narrative of Alan Turing's career, which can be simplistically summed up as 'the heroic codebreaker who was persecuted for being homosexual and killed himself as a result'.

In this book, I will show that the standard narrative is largely wrong. Alan Turing was not really a codebreaker – he spent little time on it, and few of the many achievements of Bletchley Park can be ascribed to Alan. He was no war 'hero' even if his crucial part in the design for the Bombe machine (a success story resulting from teamwork, not Marvel Comics superhero magic) enabled vital intelligence to be generated in volumes unimagined before World War Two. In fact, Alan Turing was far more than a codebreaker, and it is almost disgraceful that we allow his achievements in other fields to be overshadowed by this, and by the mis-step by which he brought down upon himself the attentions of a hostile police force, leading to his conviction for 'gross indecency'. The excessive, almost prurient attention given to Alan's trial and subsequent treatment has allowed us to define him by his sexuality; worse, we have woven a morality myth, in which Evil Forces drive an Innocent Victim into an Abyss of Despair. Alan Turing was no victim and his death was unrelated to the hormone treatment imposed upon him following his trial. We should reappraise the standard narrative and rediscover in Alan Turing the things which he himself could be proud of.

The process of rediscovery begins with Alan Turing's origins and family background. He was a child of the Empire – an Empire which was becoming technocratic and scientific while clinging to a racist, gender-biased view of different people's rightful roles in society. These things were in the background for the developmental period of his life, and it is perhaps remarkable that Alan Turing did not turn out to be racist or misogynist. Instead, he quietly supported a Jewish refugee boy from Austria and his (much older) friend from childhood, Hazel Ward, in her missionary work in Africa, as well as his frustrated scientist-manquée mother, with whom relations were rarely good. Unashamedly, I want to look at Alan Turing within the context of his family – my family; not, therefore, as the isolated Victim of the standard narrative, but as someone doing extraordinary things in a rather ordinary context. And in doing so, we can rediscover an Alan Turing who had many friends, an acid sense of humour, an irritating stammer, and an intolerance of what my grandfather called 'humbug' and these days we would call bullshit.

I am often asked what 'stories' about Alan were told at home during my childhood. The subtext of the question is an imagined family scene with crumpets toasting round the winter fire and the excuse for rose-tinted reminiscence. I am afraid my answer is a disappointment. There was no fire, and Alan Turing was not a subject for discussion. He died in 1954, and during my childhood in the following decade the circumstances of his death were still raw and not for exposure. Only when my grandmother – the author of the first, and until 1984, only, biography of Alan Turing – died in the mid 1970s did things begin to change. At the same time, the astonishing fact of Bletchley Park's successes broke news, and the possibility that Alan Turing had been involved in some way became known. My father rediscovered pride in his younger brother and, in a short chapter in one of his many unpublished books, felt able to write a counterblast to his own mother's 1959 hagiography of Alan. Alan Turing had, in a sense, been the inventor of the computer, which had earned him a Fellowship of the Royal Society – which was pretty amazing in itself – and now there was the added thrill of a key role in breaking Enigma at Bletchley Park.

That meant that Alan Turing's influence on my own life was subtle. In the early 1970s, Bletchley was still a tightly kept secret. Few people had any experience of a computer, and the knowledge of Alan Turing's contribution to computer science was limited to exactly that small group of specialists who had studied this rarefied field. But it certainly motivated me. I followed in his footsteps to Sherborne School, where it seemed strange that it was the biology building, not the computer room, that had been named after him. At least the school had a computer, which was unusual for the time.

After school, I followed Alan to King's College, Cambridge. This again was a deliberate choice: if he had gone there, that was the road to follow. And I suppose it was, partly, because of Alan's legacy that I chose to study science subjects there, though subsequently I realised that my skills probably lie elsewhere and I did not, in the end, make science my career.

In the thirty-five or so years since I left university, all that has changed. The Bletchley story, coupled with the standard narrative of Alan Turing's life story, has resonated strongly with the public. It is right, and humbling, for people to want to know more. But this is not a biography. Rather, this is about how events in Alan's background – his family, his life, and his achievements – could stimulate us to think about ourselves and our own society. Although it is Alan Turing that brings us to this reckoning, it is for us to grow his legacy.

The legacy of Alan Turing is not just about codebreaking and information security, or even his ground-laying work in computer science or biology or mathematics, though I believe he would much rather have been remembered for these things than his personal story. His story is certainly not a licence to indulge in the false nostalgia of a war won by force of intellect rather than the foul business of killing, nor even to congratulate ourselves for our modern liberalism towards homosexuality. Instead, I suggest that Alan Turing's legacy, seen in the context of his origins and achievements, is an agenda. To use his own words, 'We can only see a short distance ahead, but we can see plenty there that needs to be done.' I hope you agree, and that you will find inspiration in this mirror on the life of someone truly remarkable.

RAJ

It was daunting enough for any young man of 16 to be summoned to the Company's offices in Leadenhall Street, even if only to appear before the Committee of Shipping. The streets of London were filthy and dangerous and quite alien to someone born on a different continent. The business of the Committee was somewhat alien too, reflecting the changing nature of the Company. For it was 1791, and the office had become something more than an administrative base for a trading operation: it was turning itself into a House of Government, and within five years the classical but modest frontage would be deemed inadequately grandiose, the buildings on either side acquired, and the whole lot knocked down to be replaced by a neo-Roman temple: because that's what you need if you aspire to Empire. The young man in question was John William Turing, a junior officer in the service of the Honourable East India Company, and he was in London to hear his fate.

It's difficult to pinpoint exactly when the Turings arrived in India, but it was certainly no later than 1729, when Dr Robert Turing was appointed surgeon's mate at Fort St David, about 100 miles south of Madras. Robert and his elder brother John, sons of a minister of the Kirk, left Scotland, joining the trade boom to India. One way or another, Turings would be in India almost continuously for over 200 years, from before the birth of the Raj until the moment of its demise.[1] To my mind, Alan Turing ought to have been born in India.

Dr Robert Turing seems to have managed all right: he settled in Madras in 1753, and married the widow Mary Taylor in 1755. He had a nice if 'remote' house just to the south of the Government Garden. Its situation was not altogether convenient, since the French siege of Madras began in December 1758 with first the British, and then the French, army deciding that Dr Turing's garden was a good place to begin operations. Robert's three children survived the excitement of two armies in their yard, and then began establishing their own army of interbreeding Turings to populate Madras. To achieve that, it was necessary to import some more Turings from Scotland. A couple of cousins, active in trade, came over in the 1760s: John and William.

John Turing married one of Robert's girls, Mary, in 1773, despite being related to her at least twice over. This didn't stop them having nine more Turing children, including some called John, Robert, William and Mary, all the better to confuse the genealogists. John's brother William Turing was, as well as being a trader, employed by the East India Company. He too had a family: a wife, Nancy, and children, John (born 1774) and Margaretha (born 1783, who died while a baby). Curiously, a family history prepared in 1880 states, 'he died unmarried and without lawful issue' in 1782; and William himself is omitted from a family tree prepared in 1849. A marginal note elsewhere in the history gives a clue to these oddities, saying that John 'had a brother William … whose social relations as revealed by his will would account for [another family member] not having heard of him'. What appalling revelations could the will contain? 'Having so many Bad debts its impossible to Say how my Estate may turn out,' it says, 'therefore I leave my natural Son John William 2000 Pags my Girl Nancy 2000 Pags and Child She is big with 2000. W Turing.' William, who wrote his will on 15 November 1782, was dead by mid-January 1783, and it fell to his brother John to sort out the bequests. The estate accounts explain that cash was paid to 'the Girl Nancey or Roja Horstain in full of her Legacy left to her by the Deceased'.[2]

So that's it. William's Girl Nancy was Indian. It was an old-style partnership, one which was common enough in the early days of British presence in India, and which horrified the Victorian descendants far more than serial intermarriages with cousins. It was that same John William Turing (whose own legacy was still owed to him in December 1783, awaiting the calling-in of a number of debts, some owed by other members of the Turing family) who was in London, in 1791, appearing before the Committee of Shipping of the Honourable East India Company:

> The Chairman of the Committee acquainting the Court that John Turing who is nominated as a Cadet for Madras appears to be a Native of India; Mr Turing was called into Court, And having withdrawn; It was moved, and on the question, Resolved Unanimously, That no Person the Son of a Native Indian, shall henceforward be appointed by the Court to employment in the Civil Military or Marine Service of the Company.

The 'Honourable' Company condemned him, without the need even for a hearing, because of the colour of his skin. No more is known about my mixed-race ancestor John William Turing.

Dr Richard Wilson, a surgeon at Trichinopoly, recognised that grown-up unadopted Anglo-Indian children should not be ignored. In 1778, he wrote to the Governor and Council of the Company:

> This Class of People is sufficiently numerous to merit the Attention of Government, than which no better Arguments, I think, can be advanced to evince the Necessity of converting them into Servants of the Publick. I shall then attempt … to proceed to point in general the Methods by which this vagrant Race may be formed into an active, bold and usefull Body of People, strengthening the Hands of Dominion with a Colony of Subjects attached to the British Nation by Consanguinity, Religion, Gratitude, Language and Manners.[3]

It was for the Company to address the problem of people marooned halfway between cultures. And the Company did, although it wasn't until 1793 that the 'Cornwallis Reforms' took hold in India. This Cornwallis was the general who had surrendered at Yorktown a decade before, and when he became the first Governor-General of India, his mission was to reform the Company into a more professional civil service. To Cornwallis, this meant Europeanisation: all Indian and Anglo-Indian officials in posts worth more than £500 a year were sacked. John William Turing's treatment had been simply a foretaste of the way Empire was going to look from now on. The celebrated historian William Dalrymple has described how mixed-race children disappear gradually from wills made by the British in India in the early years of the nineteenth century. He reckons that the biggest surprise is that the existence of people like John Turing surprises us: 'It is as if the Victorians succeeded in colonizing not only India but also, more permanently, our imaginations.'[4]

So what has this gothic ramble through the cobwebs of history got to do with Alan Turing? While a recurrent theme in this book is prejudice and discrimination, it would be a little absurd to suggest that Alan Turing's life was in any way shaped by the events of 1791. But a genuine question for me is how much Alan Turing's own mindset was influenced by his Indian, or more specifically Empire, heritage. To solve this equation, we have to go forward a few decades.

The Turings seem to have been mercifully absent from India when the upheaval took place which, when I was at school, was still called 'the Indian Mutiny' (more of that Victorian brainwashing, when nowadays we recognise it to have been an uprising for independence). By the time the Turings were back on stage, the transformation of India from a trading partner to an imperial client had been completed, and the roles for them were as civil administrators of the Empire. My grandfather Julius Mathison Turing arrived in 1897 in (where else?) the Madras Province with all the requirements of a young member of the Indian Civil Service (ICS): impeccable marks in the exam, a crash-course in Tamil, and an expectation that a 20-something-year-old history student from Oxford could become the embodiment of law courts, town planning department, education ministry, water board, inland revenue and you-name-it. In this late Victorian world of spice, tweed and sweat there was no trade in sight, and certainly no mixed-race people in any position to confuse the distinction between the governors and the governed.

Julius put more than Turing genes into his sons – if my father was anything to go by, India was in the emotional DNA. John, born in India in 1908, was vocal about the civilising role of the British Empire, and when, in 1944, he had the opportunity of a war posting in Delhi, he took it without hesitation. It was the place where, far more than Britain, his heart really belonged. Still, John couldn't see the wood for the trees, on occasion. In the heyday of Empire, in 1904, the travel writer Walter Del Mar wrote, 'One of the most depressing things about India is the hopeless sadness of the people.'[5] In one sentence, he explodes the late Victorian myth of a British Empire which brings education, wealth and light to a beleaguered people. It may not have been oppression for its own sake – surely it was far more muddled than that – but it is hard, at this distance, to understand what the British in India got out of it. Today, the legacy is still mixed: without the Raj, we wouldn't have the variety of cultural influences that makes Britain an exciting place to live; without the Raj, the subcontinent wouldn't have had to endure the aftershocks of Partition which continue to reverberate even after seventy years.

Yet Alan was not part of this cultural tradition. Unlike his older brother, he had not been torn away from his native soil and sent off to wet and foggy Britain at the age of 4. Indeed, it was John Turing's fault that Alan was born in Britain and never went to India (I'm talking about my father here, not any of the other score of John Turings in the family tree). For the Turing parents decided, as many Raj families did, that the wet and fog of Britain was a healthier climate for their white children than India, and by 1912 John was getting too old to stay in India much longer.

So Alan was born in London, and for the whole of his childhood he lived with a British foster family when not at boarding school. So we may legitimately ask what relevance the Raj has to his life story. Perhaps not much, but it is constantly there in the background, and our (mis)perceptions of Alan Turing can go further astray if we do not recognise its influence. For children of the Raj like Alan, the Empire was always there: it did not need to be commented on, explained away or analysed, or even thought about. It was just there, as the corpuscles that colour your blue British blood red. In practical terms, this showed itself in small ways, in the natural order of things for those surrounded by servants and deference, where the deference was not so much expected as an inherited characteristic. Abrupt dealings with waiters and ticket-office staff; impatience expressed in an upper-class accent; an amateurish cluelessness when it came to ordinary things like making a pot of tea. Sometimes, when we hear of Alan Turing's dealings with other people, we treat them as idiosyncrasies rather than hangovers from the old Empire. He may have been less Indianised than his brother, but his style may have been more normal than we like to admit.

The Raj was an unlikely seedbed for Alan Turing's interest in science and mathematics. Indeed, Julius Turing's passions for history and literature were a world away from all that, though happily adopted by his older son John. Nor can we expect to find the germination of Alan's interests in his foster home: Colonel Ward and his extended army family, who were broadminded enough to tolerate and indulge – but not to plan – the boy's slightly un-Empire, boundary-breaking counter-current of experiment and enquiry. So we must turn elsewhere for the source of all that.

A clue may be found back in India. Julius Turing arrived in Madras too late to be married off to one of the multiple Turing cousins of the 1760s, and an association like that of William Turing's, with a local girl, was out of the question in the 1890s. Eligible girls had to be found among the white Raj, and they were rare commodities. According to Jane Austen, you would need both luck and a fortune of £7,000 to captivate a baronet; Julius Turing was not a baronet (though his cousin

Sir Robert was), so maybe the price was lower. And luck played its part, in the form of the failure of the Fishing Fleet.

The Fishing Fleet was made up of girls who could not find a husband at home and so were packed off to hook someone desperate in the torrid climes of the subcontinent. The picture is a cake mix of glamour, fortune-hunting, survival and snobbery, and as with many stories encapsulated in an acid phrase there is a bit – a tiny bit – of truth in it. Girls like Ethel Stoney, who had been born in India and educated back home, might have had better prospects in the social circles of the Raj. So she was shipped back to her father's house, to leave visiting cards and attend late Victorian balls, stay out of the midday sun, and eat British food, all in an atmosphere of polite vapidity, since this was how fishing should be done. But the baronet's cousin was always on tour, as my father recorded:

> It was a royal progress. He dwelt in a vast marquee divided into three sections – office, living quarters and bedroom. The advance party went ahead with tents, cooks and condiments; the syce was at hand to hold the pony's head, the bearer stood by with a clean shirt and a sundowner. When he returned from the early morning ride breakfast was ready; the punkah wallah was there to keep him as cool as might be and the peon was squatting nearby to take any message at his bidding. But let those who have never felt the baking heat of India on their backs, nor had to write with a blotter under the wrist to soak up the perspiration, mock such elementary aids to survival.[6]

Alan Turing's mother had come to India on the Fishing Fleet, but the balls and visiting cards were no way to meet Alan Turing's father. It wasn't going to be, because the social strata, even in the tiny community of the white Raj in the Madras Province, would conspire against it even if the endless tours did not. The story involves Irishness and science; to unravel this mystery, we need to travel up into the hills, and because we are in India, it is fitting that we should do so by train.

The journey from Madras up to Coonoor, situated up in the Nilgiri Hills, is one of 500km as the crow flies, and a lot further by train. According to the timetable, it takes seven hours to get to Coimbatore, but for the final leg you have to switch to the scenic, UNESCO-listed Nilgiri Mountain Railway, featured in movies such as *A Passage to India*. The railway is the only rack railway in India, and it was not a straightforward operation when the line opened in 1899: rockfalls almost filling the cuttings, destruction of bridges, corners too tight for the flanges

The Gardens of the Chief Engineer's residence, in about 1909 – the small figure in white is Alan's brother John, with his ayah. (Author's collection)

on the wheels.[7] The difficulties had to be surmounted, as it was important to the British to have this line: the hill station at Ootacamund was the hot-season seat of government of the Province, where it was possible to wear tweed in relative comfort; and on the way to Ooty, in Coonoor, the residence of the Chief Engineer of the Madras Railways was situated.

The British introduced the railways into India, maybe to foster trade, maybe to assert control; Indian railways, often seen as the positive legacy of Empire, were inseparable from the idea of Empire. More than anything, railways defined not just India, but the British Empire. Railway-building extended far beyond the parts of the map that were coloured pink. But young British public-school men, like Julius Turing, who were now ruling India, were not involved with the dirty business of railways. The railways were the province of the Anglo-Indians. A hundred years after the civil service door had slammed shut on John William Turing in 1791, Anglo-Indians had found in the Indian railway system a semi-detached world which they could make their own, at last becoming Dr Wilson's 'usefull body of People, strengthening the Hands of Dominion' in the different occupations of driving trains, signalling, engineering and administration.

The position of the professionals in charge was, similarly, an invisible notch below that of the 'heaven-born' ICS on their semi-royal progresses. The upper echelons of the engineers may have been white, but it was clear that the demi-monde of the Anglo-Indian railways were not *quite* like *us*. Thus, while the summer government of the ICS was in Ooty, the Chief Engineer was in Coonoor. No chance, then, for the daughter of E.W. Stoney – who by 1899 had become the Chief Engineer of the Madras Railway (including its troublesome branch to Coonoor and Ootacamund) – to mix in circles where she could meet an eligible non-baronet of the ICS class. But a damned good catch, from Stoney's perspective, if something like that were possible. Climbing up to the position of Chief Engineer was, for a home-educated boy from County Tipperary, something of an achievement. To quote his grandson John again:

> The Stoneys are a hard-headed lot, with a bent for engineering, mathematics and practical affairs and – one might as well admit it – an eye for number one and instant recognition of the importance of money in this second-rate world. My maternal grandfather happily combined these characteristics. By his own industry and resource and a talent of invention he climbed the ladder to become Chief Engineer of the Madras Railway, amassed a considerable fortune and a C.I.E. [Companion of the Order of the Indian Empire] and lived in a large, comfortable house in the Nilgiris. (I must not complain of that, for I was born there.)

In this short passage, John's distaste for science, and for self-betterment, rise to the surface; it's no surprise that Alan's differing interests might clash with John's professional-class lifestyle in later life, pushing the boys apart.

Hard-headed or not, Edward Stoney had the kind of brains for algebra which won him the engineering scholarship at Queen's College, Galway, coming first in the final examinations in which students competed from all three of the Queen's Colleges in Ireland. Transported to India as a fourth-class engineer in 1866, Stoney constructed bridges crossing vast rivers – the Chittravati Bridge, with nineteen spans of 42m, was built to replace a bridge partly destroyed in 1874 by a flood, and was an interesting enough bridge to find its way into the Proceedings of the Institution of Civil Engineers.[8]

the Nilgiri Railway was under his supervision, but the permanent way Mr. Stoney. was very well and carefully maintained in every way, and it had been well laid originally. A good deal of trouble was caused by rapid wear of engine-tires, which cut away the inner flanges of the outside rails on curves, so that they looked quite rough, as if

Fig. 1.

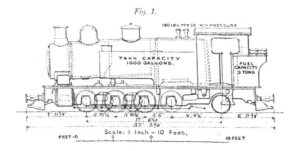

shorn. The use of a fine water-jet prevented this, and the rails became quite smooth again, but he understood the use of such jets had been given up, as the engine-drivers thought it interfered with

Fig. 2.

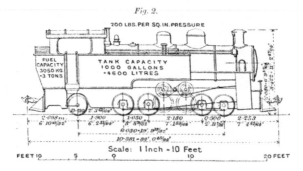

adhesion. The following Table showed the great increase in size, weight, and power of the four classes of engines used. Engines of classes " P " and " X " were illustrated in Figs. 1 and 2. The line between Coonoor and Ootacamund was an adhesion one with a ruling gradient of 1 in 40.

E 2

Nilgiri Line locomotives, with the rack-drives half concealed. From a paper by E.W. Stoney in the *Minutes of the Proceedings of the ICE*.

Building interesting bridges does not make you an interesting person, and the double handicap of Irishness and being insufficiently Raj does not set up your daughter for an Austenesque match. So it was on a ship – going the opposite way from the Fishing Fleet, eastabout to America – that Julius Turing met Ethel. Jane Austen might not have approved the manner of courtship ('in Japan my father took my mother out to dinner and bade the Japanese waiter to bring beer and keep on bringing beer until I tell you to stop') but it worked; after a lecture to Ethel from Mr Stoney on the subject of 'bickering in shebeens' and the risks of life with a drunkard, the match was approved. Julius Turing did not touch beer except when courting or fishing; he was ICS, and even if his life insurance of £500 was not quite the requisite £7,000 prescribed by Miss Austen, he had not committed the inexcusable offence of being completely penniless. So Ethel Stoney became a memsahib, and the Turing boys were born into a strange mix of ICS and engineering.

Given the overwhelming cultural background of the Empire and its bizarre assumption that good government was fostered by a classical education, it is somewhat unlikely that Alan was able to develop as a mathematician and scientist. One of his favourite books seems to have been Samuel Butler's *Erewhon*, in which the educational system of the Victorians is lampooned: in Colleges of Unreason, students graduate if they can translate into a dead language of no current practical worth. The theory of education which holds that a study of Latin and Greek is essential persisted right up to the mid-1970s, when at Sherborne School it was unthinkable for any student not to at least attempt Latin O-level. You needed classics to be an administrator or manager, and to produce such creatures is what the Great Public Schools were for. One wonders how Alan Turing escaped being channelled towards that fate; certainly,

Sherborne School (of which more in the next chapter) went to great lengths to ensure he did get a School Certificate pass in Latin. It may have been that Alan had the Stoneys' bent for engineering and mathematics in his blood; whether it was Grandpa Stoney's direct influence is more questionable.

With his Edwardian beard, watch chain, dignity and concern for money, and his deeply dull conversation, Edward Stoney did not endear himself to his grandsons John and Alan. Any forthcoming visit caused much family tension, with everyone required to be on their best behaviour – an injunction doomed to fail as the grandchildren set out for revenge:

> When my brother Alan and I were much older and [grandpa] Stoney was well into his 80s, we behaved very *badly* and invented a game which relieved the tedium of my grandfather's stories. He had about 20 in all and we had all heard them dozens of times. So the game was for one of us to get him started on story A and then the other had to divert him and get him started on B; then when he was well started on that the promoter of B would try to keep him on that, whilst the promoter of A tried to get him back to A or on to story C.

That is probably enough to put paid to any suggestion that Alan Turing's mathematical aptitude was stimulated by his engineer grandfather. But it's possible – just possible – that the scientific inclinations of the Stoneys filtered into his life by a different process of family osmosis. Alan's attitudes came from his father's side, but his talents from his mother's side. We should not be seduced by the father's surname, and it would be reckless to ignore the influence of the women in Alan's life.

X-RAY

It was probably inevitable that I would end up at Sherborne School, because that's where Alan had been educated, and my father considered that it was his own intervention which had brought Alan to Sherborne in 1926. John had been taught at Marlborough College, and his tales of lavatorial horror – including a ghastly communal-flushing arrangement where all cubicles were serviced at once – coupled with a traditional regimen had been enough to convince my grandparents that Marlborough would break Alan. Marlborough was all very well for instilling into would-be rulers of the Empire the psychological grit and sanitary preparedness they would need to carry the Crown's message to the remotest corners of the map. But science was not on the curriculum, and Marlborough's saving grace, an inspired teacher of English who instilled in his charges a lifelong affection for the poetry of John Keats, was not the sort of thing that was going to appeal to Alan Turing.

We'll come back to Sherborne shortly, but it was clear that Alan Turing had already shown an interest in mathematics and all aspects of science during his childhood, and his early schoolteachers had seen this aptitude in him; the question was whether, in the early 1920s, it was possible to bring out his talents.

Ethel Turing was going to take the credit for it: her own biography, first published in 1959, is full of incidents from Alan's childhood where his scientific prowess was apparently evident, but she doesn't explain why Alan, who had successfully sat the entrance examination for Marlborough, went to Sherborne instead.[1] It was, in fact, modernism: Sherborne had adopted the 'modern' curriculum as an alternative to the traditional Empire preparation of classics, scripture and sport. Being 'modern' meant courses in physics and chemistry and more than a bit of mathematics, which was obviously a sound choice for Alan. But that doesn't explain how a boy, the son of Raj parents growing up in a military foster family, could be fitted culturally into something as unsuitable, not to mention career-limiting, as a scientific education. There were forces other than those of Empire at work.

Alan's grandfather E.W. Stoney could have been a driving force, but, as we have seen, his influence over the grandchildren was limited, and by the time schooling decisions were being made he was in retirement in Bournemouth, while the Turing parents were still in India. Nevertheless, Ethel wanted her children, and the world, to know that the connection with the Stoneys was important: she had herself grown up in Ireland, where their reputation was strong. In her book, she mentions particularly G.J. Stoney, FRS, and there's an attractive hand-drawn portrait of him, done by his daughter Gertrude, in an album of photographs she prepared for Alan. (The equivalent album, prepared by her for John, has many photos of India but does not include this portrait.) The album was put together years before Alan's interests became apparent, so we can infer that G.J. Stoney was an important influence.

George Johnstone Stoney was a very distant cousin. For Ethel to go back up the family tree to a common ancestor, it was a climb of five generations to George Stoney, who had died in 1787. George had three sons: Ethel's great-great-grandfather Thomas, his younger brother James (who was G.J. Stoney's grandfather), and by far the most notorious Stoney of all time, Andrew Robinson Stoney Bowes. The Stoney Bowes story is too much fun to risk an inadequate summary here, so suffice it to say that he deceived a countess into marrying him and then locked her in a wardrobe – and that's just chapter one. Ethel did not put a picture of Stoney Bowes in her albums for John and Alan. Second-cousin-twice-removed George Johnstone Stoney had fame for much more positive reasons than Stoney Bowes, and it's clear that she was proud to be related to the one, if not the other.

I am often asked if I am 'proud' of Alan Turing and his achievements. I thought pride was one of the seven deadly sins; the word conjures up an impression of self-satisfied basking in someone else's hard work, and pretending to be better than others for no good reason. If this is what people mean, which I doubt, pride is a very uncomfortable sentiment. To check up on my pride, I looked up the word in the *Shorter Oxford Dictionary*, and it didn't make me feel much better:

> **Proud. I.1.** Having a high or lofty opinion of oneself; valuing oneself highly on account of one's position, rank, attain-ments, possessions, etc. Usu. in bad sense.

Horrors. To share a surname does not make me a lofty person; to value oneself highly on the basis of someone else's attain-ments seems downright dishonest. Meaning two is a bit better:

> Highly sensible of, or elated by, some honour done to one.

That's more like it. I am certainly honoured to bear the surname – it would have been better to have earned the honour, but I'm highly sensible of it. It's either a blessing or a disappointment to have received a mix of genes which may be shared with Alan Turing; but while he was someone to be inspired by, even to aspire to catch up with, my own abilities are in a rather different sphere. Anyhow, I think that it was a kind of sensibility to the honour that might possibly rub off on her that Ethel felt about her famous kinsman, George Johnstone Stoney.

G.J. Stoney was minor Anglo-Irish gentry but with a strong Enlightenment streak which encouraged scientific enquiry. He was born in 1826 – slightly after the peak of intellectual and practical breakthroughs in England typified by the Darwins, Wedgwoods and Watts, but sharing the spirit of gentleman-amateurs who could dirty themselves with philosophical experimentation in their backyard outbuildings, financed by inherited cash. The problem for G.J. Stoney was that there was not a great deal of family cash, and when he came of age in 1847, Ireland was in the middle of the potato famine. But the Earl of Rosse lived not far from the Stoneys at Parsonstown in the King's County (these days, it's Birr in County Offaly), and the noble lord had just built a 72in reflector telescope in one of his backyard outbuildings. Stoney, with his BA from Trinity College, Dublin, became the Earl's astronomical assistant. This provided a practical grounding which, together with his academic credentials, enabled him in a few years to apply for the position of Professor of Natural Philosophy at the Queen's College, Galway.[2]

From there, Stoney went on to a distinguished academic career, becoming a Fellow of the Royal Society in 1861; his enduring contribution to science came in 1874 at a meeting of the British Association for the Advancement of Science in

Belfast, when he presented a paper, 'On the physical units of nature', in which he suggested the existence of an indivisible unit of negative electrical charge – something he then called the 'electrine'. It is to G.J. Stoney that we owe the concept of the electron. No doubt this was the thing which impressed Ethel – but it is Stoney's immediate family which impress me, and probably gave Ethel a glimpse of what might have been, if she had grown up in a different part of Ireland, or in a different branch of the family, and not been dragged by the railways into the Raj.

What G.J. Stoney had done, when not proposing indivisibility of charge in sub-atomic particles, was to allow his daughters to choose and pursue whatever careers they wanted. There were three: Edith, born in 1869; Florence, in 1870; and Gertrude, in 1871. There should have been a fourth, but the tragedy of George Johnstone Stoney was that his wife and new baby both died as a result of the complications and crudeness of Victorian childbirth, in 1872. This left Stoney as a single parent of the three girls and their two older brothers. This situation, in ordinary Victorian conditions, should have led to the children being fostered by some female relative, but Stoney took over the parenting, and his example was, accordingly, one which all the children, regardless of gender, could feel able to follow.

The usual education for middle-class Anglo-Irish girls was at Alexandra College in Dublin. There it was possible to learn not just the ladylike subjects of classics and history, but to get stuck into mathematics and philosophy. In a few years' time, Ethel Stoney would go there; but G.J. Stoney either couldn't afford the fees or wanted to oversee the girls' development himself, so they were taught at home. Gertrude never wanted to be a scientist, but Edith and Florence were fascinated by the microscope, the telescope, the bicycle repairs and the chemistry of photography going on in the house and its backyard. None of this was particularly ladylike, especially the cycling, which had to take place in public. By the late 1880s, home schooling wasn't equal to the girls' needs, and both Edith and Florence were enrolled in the Royal College for Science for Ireland, to prepare for higher education.

Florence seems to have determined on a career in medicine. This – to some degree – was a pathway available to women even in the 1880s. We should probably recall that even in the later years of Victoria's reign, medicine was a fairly primitive affair, given the state of knowledge about infectious disease and bio-chemistry. What general practitioners did was diagnosis and provide comfort, rather than cures, and this was something which women could do without loss of gentility. Florence won a place to study at the London School of Medicine for Women, which had been established in 1874.

Edith was probably never cut out to be a doctor. Throughout her life she seems to have had slightly prickly relations with her work colleagues, and she may have lacked the bedside manner of her sister. But this didn't matter, since Edith wanted to study mathematics. She was accepted by Newnham College, Cambridge, and went there in 1890. Cambridge was a hostile environment for women students in the 1890s, never mind immigrant women from Ireland. In 1897, thousands of old boys descended on the city to participate in a vote on the question of whether the university should award degrees to women. Special trains were laid on to get the boater-wearing voters up from London and ladders were erected so that the windows of the Senate House, where the voting took place, could serve as additional doorways. The business was controversial enough for there to be opposition to the invasion of voters – eggs were thrown and fireworks were let off – but the motion was defeated by 1,707 to 661.[3]

Edith, then, wasn't going to be allowed to graduate from Cambridge. Her exam results weren't spectacular; even if they had been, there was the question of what she could do, as a young woman with a mathematics non-degree, even one from Cambridge. The obvious career path was teaching. So, briefly, Edith became a physics teacher at Cheltenham Ladies' College, where distant cousin Ethel's sister, Evie, was a student. Ethel was to follow in 1898.

Cheltenham Ladies' College, run by the formidable Miss Beale, had no patience with the idea that being ladylike required an exclusive focus on needlework and singing and other feminine accomplishments. Physics teachers like Edith were needed because girls could be just as good at science as boys. Ethel Stoney arrived at Cheltenham just too late to be taught by her cousin Edith, who had moved on, but she did achieve a first class in the University of London's matriculation examination for science in 1899. Perhaps Ethel might be destined for science herself?

But no, Ethel went on to the Sorbonne in Paris – a prestigious school if ever there was one, but it was to polish up her French and to get herself prepared with those skills needed if you were destined for the Fishing Fleet. The scientific baton of the Stoneys would, instead, continue to be borne by Ethel and Florence. Florence got her medical degree, became an anatomy demonstrator, and built up a general medical practice. After leaving Cheltenham, Edith was encouraged by Florence to apply for the newly created post of lecturer in physics at the London School of Medicine for Women, where Florence was anatomy demonstrator. Edith beat the male contender on the shortlist and began teaching physics to would-be lady medics.

Medicine was coming along. Florence's own training had involved ophthalmology, paediatrics, anaesthesia – and a developing sense of gender discrimination, noting that the opportunities for girls to do sports and exercise were far more limited than those for boys. The big break for both Florence and Edith came in 1902, when the Royal Free Hospital bought a Röntgen Ray apparatus – that is to say, an X-ray machine. X-rays were lighting the path of progress, but as with other innovations, they were still rather hit-and-miss. You could use X-rays, like electrical shocks, for experimental radiotherapy, as well as for seeing invisible things like foreign bodies and dislocated joints. The operator of the equipment was subjected to high and dangerous levels of radiation – burnt skin was not uncommon – and the equipment itself was temperamental and difficult. Still, Miss (Florence) Stoney was appointed as electrician on an annual salary of 20 guineas to supervise the new machine. She was the first woman radiologist in Britain. As a physics lecturer, Edith was getting £100 a year at this time; either way, in 1902, women scientists were good value for money. And as physicist in residence, Edith became involved in the maintenance of Florence's X-ray machine.

Edith wasn't easy to work with: she wanted perfection in her arrangements; she spoke her mind in direct terms (on suffrage (for), on physics (for), on sexism (against), on Irish Home Rule (against)); compromise and pragmatism don't seem to have been part of her make-up. It was also harder for people to understand Edith's role: the idea of a professional woman scientist was odd enough, but to place her in a hospital setting meant that she must be a doctor (no, she wasn't) or a nurse (definitely not), so she was perhaps nothing at all. Her influence was, therefore, less than her education and experience should have merited, and there were run-ins with those in authority, possibly less able than her but more powerful, and bouts of unemployment – in contrast with Florence's more steady progression.

The apogee of both women's careers came about with World War One and the use of X-ray machines – and a mobile X-ray unit in a van (insufficiently rugged, according to Edith) – to deal with battlefield casualties across Europe. During the course of the war, the sisters found themselves variously posted to Belgium, France, Greece and Serbia, as well as England. Both were decorated for their service: Edith received the Serbian Order of St Sava and the French Croix de Guerre; Florence was given the OBE and received the 1914 Mons Star. Both women received the standard War and Victory medals in addition. A lasting tragedy of World War One is that women who had broken the glass ceiling were firmly put back under it once the

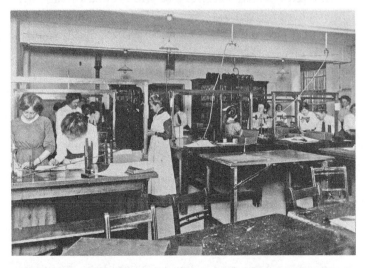

Edith Stoney (centre) teaching physics to women medical students shortly before World War One. (Reproduced by kind permission of the Royal Free London NHS Foundation Trust)

war was over. Florence went back to general practice and Edith to teaching.

By this time, Ethel Stoney – now Ethel Turing, a memsahib and long-distance mother – was about as far away from practical science as it is possible to be. Still, there had been that possibility of a similar career when she was a teenager, which only the drive of her own father could have achieved. But it was too unconventional even to bear a moment's thought for E.W. Stoney, and probably never even got discussed. What happened, instead, was like the growth of a plant kept in the dark, colourless and constantly striving for light which isn't there. The might-have-been exemplified by G.J. Stoney's daughters was a powerful influence on Alan Turing.

Alan's relationship with his mother has sometimes been overlooked because the story of Alan's relationship with Christopher Morcom, his tragic Sherborne friend, has a more powerful appeal and a hint of homoeroticism. But if you look at Ethel's own biography of her famous son, you might get a different impression. We should take a moment to consider how they really related to one another.

Ethel spent World War One in India; Alan and my father were fostered for ten years with the Ward family in St Leonards-on-Sea, and later, after a plea from my father for a change, for a year or so with the Reverend Rollo Meyer at Watton-at-Stone in Hertfordshire. In 1925 there was a much bigger change. A pointless question of priority for promotion led my grandfather to resign in a huff from the Indian Civil Service at the age of 51, so Julius 'condemned himself to more than twenty years of frustration, disillusion and boredom', according to my father. Julius and Ethel returned to Europe. Not to Britain – at least, not yet – but to Dinard in the Département of Ille-et-Vilaine, just opposite St-Malo where the Channel Islands ferry docks.

It is no coincidence that the annual 'French Trip' in the Easter holidays from my prep school went to Dinard: it was the 1920s retirement town of choice for British expats, with a public outdoor swimming bath, an attractive sandy beach on which one could attempt to play hockey, an Anglican church, together with a suitably English climate (wet), and most important of all, low taxation. What had been good enough for Julius Turing in 1925 was still good enough for Fernden School forty-five years later.

In 1925 the Marlborough versus Sherborne secondary school-ing choices were being made for Alan, and it was also the time when long-distance parenting was brought to an end. Alan's mother could now take an interest in what had once appealed to her, in those far-off days in Ireland. A son who was excited by science dangled the prospect of rekindling her own interests.

This was all very well, but Alan's relationship with his mother was one of biology, not emotion. It was different for John: during whose infant years Mother had been a constant, if somewhat regal, presence. Coming to England in 1912 had, for John, been a process of deracination; for Alan, it was noth-ing of the sort, since his nuclear family had been the Wards. In Dinard, he was having to adjust to the idea that real parents, rather than the laissez-faire Meyers, might wish to exercise influence, even control, over their teenage son's behaviour.

We get little detail on this from the written record, and even that is the victim of censorship. These days, I spend a part of my time looking into historical government archives trying to find out details of secret codebreaking operations. How gov-ernments (of various nations) have chosen to edit, select and redact what is made available to researchers is often incom-prehensible, and much of what you learn is that you can only see part of the picture. The same is true with regard to Alan

Turing. To her credit, Alan's mother gave a collection – or maybe I should say a selection – of Alan's letters to her to King's College, Cambridge, in the 1960s, and from these we can see a part of his picture. But Sara (as she had decided to be called after World War Two) chose the letters which would illustrate Alan's innate scientific genius, not those which would show him as an annoying, ordinary teenager; and we only have his side of the correspondence. Nonetheless, we can shine the light sideways and, perhaps, infer a few things.

For one thing, Alan's mother was constantly badgering him – and let's admit that this does not make her unusual – about things like tidiness, cleanliness, diligent attention to studies and so forth. That much comes out in her own book. Yet there's a gap of four years, after Alan's letters about his first arrival at Sherborne (in itself something of a remarkable achievement, as, not yet 14, Alan rode his bicycle in defiance of the General Strike all the way from Southampton in order to get there). Then his letters are predominantly concerned with scientific subjects, such as quantum theory, chemistry, mathematics and astronomy. Alan was choosing neutral ground for correspondence: topics which Ethel could seek to engage with, and, with some foggy vestige of her own education, try to follow what was going on.

I may be reading more into this than the record will bear, but the sense I have – borne out by my father's own rollercoaster relationship with his parents – is that Ethel spent much of her life after the Raj trying to get closer to her younger son than he would allow; resuming her interest in scientific questions was a way to engage with Alan when ordinary chit-chat was out of the question. What is less convincing is to imagine that Alan himself was enthusiastic about all this; tolerant, maybe, some of the time. What was legitimate concern on her part

Alan Turing when at Sherborne. (Reproduced by kind permission of
Sherborne School)

might have come across as interfering or even controlling to him. Alan's relationship with Christopher Morcom's energetic, practical and impartial mother was much more relaxed, and even affectionate.

Alan Turing's relationships with women deserve more attention than they have generally received. Sherborne, of course, was an all-male society. (Even when I got there in 1974, there was only one woman on the teaching staff outside the Music School – a young woman from Bavaria, whose job was to teach me the rudiments of German; that she failed was not her fault. Now the place is transformed, and while it's still a boys' school, the teaching staff is thoroughly mixed gender, so the boys do not grow up imagining that women are a race apart.) So was King's College, Cambridge. Two years in the United States gave Alan some mixed company, though Princeton itself was another men's club. Bletchley Park could have been one more, except that the desperate need for codebreaking staff drove Alastair Denniston, the head of the organisation there, to abandon his preference that vacancies should not be filled by women. It was only at Bletchley, and later at Manchester, that Alan met women in the workplace.

The reports are not uniformly good: Alan didn't seem to know what to do or say. As he was shy and uncomfortable with ordinary social banter, the only way for him to have anything resembling a relationship was to stick to the intellectual plane. At Bletchley – where, contrary to modern myth, there was a vibrant, confident group of high-achieving women doing code-breaking and analysis – it was possible for women to be seen as humans and of equal status (more or less) with men. Although 'if anyone asked us what we did, we were to say that we were secretaries', to the insiders at Bletchley it was quite apparent that women were quite as capable as the men.[4] Thus Alan

Turing was able to indulge, probably for the first time in his life, in conversation with a female of the species who was not his own mother.

This, of course, evolved into Alan's short engagement with Joan Clarke, whose own reputation as one of Britain's foremost women cryptanalysts, after the war as well as during it, has become subducted into a footnote to the tale of Alan Turing. Joan wasn't, even if she had been allowed by the Official Secrets Act, the sort of person to do publicity, and it is unfortunate that the world of women at Bletchley (of whom Joan Clarke ought to be something of a role model, if not a champion) has become so distorted over the years. In part, it's because the dozens of women recruited for fully professional jobs were called things like 'clerical staff', which masked their real, senior, functions; in part, it's because the professional women were outnumbered by the huge intake of even younger women recruited to operate the Bombe machinery and do other junior roles, thereby encouraging a narrative of men-doing-codebreaking and women-doing-menial-work which is only half true. History has something to do with this, too: the experience of World War One unhappily repeated itself as Bletchley Park disbanded, with the women codebreakers – forbidden to describe their wartime jobs and capabilities – disappearing into domestic greyness in a male-dominated post-war reactionary Britain, where everything from potatoes to intellect was on ration.

Which brings us to the question of women in technology. Alan Turing's other significant encounter with women in the workplace was when he was taken on by M.H.A. Newman in 1948. This was when Alan was appointed Deputy Director of the Royal Society Computing Machine Laboratory which Newman had set up; Newman also recruited some laboratory assistants to help with the complex process of programming.

Newman wasn't going to appoint anyone who was an intellectual slouch; the recruits to help Alan were Audrey Bates (who was studying for her MSc, supervised by Alan) and Cicely Popplewell (a mathematics pseudo-graduate from Cambridge; Cambridge still didn't give degrees to women in 1942, when she should have graduated). Alan didn't relate to them very well: there was too much of an age gap, too much of a seniority gap, too much inequality all round. Audrey and Cicely were relieved when Alan was not in the lab and they had the place to themselves. The remarkable thing about this is not so much that Alan was the impossible and distant boss – who has not experienced that? – but that Audrey and Cicely were in technical employment at all. Still, at this time, Alan had a friendly long-distance relationship with another student, Beatrice Worsley, who was probably the first person in the world to study for a doctorate in computer science. We will meet Beatrice again, but I think she and Alan got on well because she had a ready and wry wit which put them on the same wavelength; maybe, having grown up in America and Canada, she was less class conscious and saw Alan less as the product of Empire which he could sometimes seem.

The post-war trajectory of women in technological roles is unedifying. Women with vital technical skills learned during and immediately after the war were steadily drained out of the workforce by a system which demanded that men be breadwinners (therefore paid more, given more seniority) and women be homemakers (therefore fired, or expected to 'retire' when they got married or became pregnant) – with the result that there was an artificial, and largely imaginary, talent famine in computer science by the mid-1960s. Unemployed women programmers were unable to get suitable work, and employers were at their wits' end, unable to find men to fill their vacancies.

The cultural belief that programming is something for men, and unsuitable for women, was burned in during the years of Harold Wilson's 'White Heat of the Technological Revolution', and remains stubbornly in place today.[5]

Cambridge eventually got round to giving degrees to women in 1948, and Cicely Popplewell got her overdue MA in 1949. Still, the gender imbalance persisted well into the late twentieth century. I went to Cambridge in 1979, when most 'men's' colleges had begun to admit women. Trinity College first allowed women students in that year, but there is a tale of one female student who showed up there before the start of term to be told by the porters that the college did not admit women.[6] Sometimes social change is, literally, incredible.

In some fields, the opportunities for women are still no better. Whether it's because engineering, computer science and physics are considered to be 'hard' subjects or 'unsuitable' for girls (I am not sure which is worse), girls who do well in their GCSEs in science or maths are under-represented relative to boys at A-level and university in these subjects.[7] Girls may also be put off studying these subjects because they fear being the only girl in the class. The imbalance gets more entrenched further on. A woman professor from Cambridge who is also a 'Turing Fellow' of the Alan Turing Institute lamented in 2020 that women miss out on the fun of being involved in artificial intelligence and related fields because of this.[8]

Back at all-boys Sherborne, it is gratifying that mathematics and science are now taught by women as well as men; one hopes that the students leave school free of the belief that these subjects are impossible for women. There is also an inelegant building there bearing the name of Alan Turing. Although it is without much architectural distinction, it is almost certainly the first school building, and quite likely the first building anywhere, to have been named in his honour. It was finished in 1966 and sits awkwardly between the honey-coloured stone buildings, both those of Alan Turing's time and the modern laboratories built in the year 2000. What was odd about it in the 1970s was not so much its architecture – there were lots of far worse school buildings in Sherborne then – but the fact that this was a building in which biology was taught.

At around the time the building was dedicated, my grandmother Sara donated a handful of Alan Turing memorabilia to the school, which – possibly because the obscurity of Alan Turing, among the non-notables after whom the school's other buildings are named, could be taken for granted – was poorly guarded. There was a brief flurry of interest in these things in January 2020, when it was reported in Boulder, Colorado, that legal proceedings had been initiated for the

The Alan Turing Laboratories at Sherborne. (Reproduced by kind permission of Sherborne School)

recovery of seventeen items, including a miniature of Alan Turing's OBE medal, allegedly stolen from Sherborne School in 1984. The 127-page complaint sets out the plot of the little drama:

> 6. A woman named Ms Julia Mathison Turing ('Ms. Turing') had contacted the University of Colorado. Ms Turing stated that she had items relating to Alan Mathison Turing ('Alan Turing'). Alan Turing was a British mathematician and pioneer of theoretical computer science and artificial intelligence. Ms Turing offered to loan the items to the University of Colorado for display.
>
> 7. As is customary at the University of Colorado when historical items are offered for display, a member of the University of Colorado researched the particular items being offered and discovered that they were likely stolen from the Sherborne School in Dorset, England, a school that Alan Turing attended as a youth.
>
> 8. Ms Turing had represented herself as a relative of Alan Turing when she contacted the University of Colorado in 2018.
>
> 9. The Director of Special Collections, Archives and Preservation at the University of Colorado determined that Ms Turing had not always gone by the name 'Turing' and was unable to find any familial link between Ms Turing and Alan Turing.[9]

That year, 1984, marked the beginning of wider knowledge of Alan Turing's life story, and the tragi-comic series of events relating to the objects at Sherborne School – objects of only limited interest to academic researchers, it should be said – is just one spin-off from the fame which he has come to acquire.

In the 1960s and 1970s, Alan Turing's name was barely known outside academic circles of higher mathematics and computer science. Nowadays, it seems, people want to bear his name as well as to possess his things.

In those earlier days, computers were monstrous mainframes, programmed in a species of esoteric algebra – wonderful nonetheless, and something every school pupil could be inspired by. If Alan Turing was going to be associated with anything, surely, it would be the invention of the computer – so the decision to name the biology building after him might seem, even now, to be slightly perverse. By the 1970s, Sherborne had acquired a computer for teaching purposes: an old Burroughs machine equipped with a useful 'panic button' for use when it got stuck in an endless loop, typified by vomiting out reams of fanfold paper printed with only a zero every few lines. Sixth formers were trained to program it, in four-digit hexadecimal machine code, of which I can remember little except that EB02 meant 'advance paper two lines'. (Now I come to think about it, that code was probably the cause of the pile of fanfold paper and my dependency on the panic button.) But the computer was unceremoniously lodged in a dingy room under the staircase leading up to the chapel, nowhere near the new building called the Turing Block.

In those days, if Alan Turing's name was unknown to the vast majority of people, his contribution to unlocking the code of developmental biology was wholly buried – something which still remains a secret to many. The choice of Turing's name for the biology building was wholly appropriate, and even now it is a good choice to prompt the question which was in my mind in the 1970s: what has Alan Turing got to do with biology? His work on morphogenesis seems never to have gripped the public imagination in the way that his other achievements do, and the question why is one to which we shall return. Nowadays, we honour Alan Turing as a codebreaker and the founder of computer science, but in 1966 computer science was no more a school subject than codebreaking. Biology it had to be. But it wasn't in biology or codebreaking that Alan Turing made the greatest impact on history.

Google Scholar lists the citations in academic papers of works by preceding academics. As you might expect, papers written by Alan Turing get cited fairly often. Fashions change, so the top three papers change places periodically; in 2020 they were:

'Computing Machinery and Intelligence' (over 13,500 citations).
'The Chemical Basis of Morphogenesis' (over 13,000 citations).
'On Computable Numbers' (over 11,500 citations).

The first of these is the paper which sets out the so-called 'Turing test' to determine whether a machine is thinking. The second is the biology paper, so the work Alan did in this field is belatedly achieving recognition. The mathematical paper which laid the foundations of what is 'computable' is, surprisingly, in third place, despite having spawned an entire genre of mathematical research. In 1935, when Alan Turing invented the subject, what was computable was what could be done by people using mechanical adding machines and robotically following a given set of instructions. These people were called 'computers', and it is an everlasting shame that in the interwar period it was only women who were recruited for a job which obliged them to behave like robots. Yet there seems to be a paradox in the two top papers by Alan Turing which concern computation: one of them defines the unthinking robotic process of 'computability', and the other one argues that machines can think. Surely these things cannot both be true?

COMPUTE

It came as something of a surprise to the Turings that Alan won a scholarship to Cambridge. John, his brother, described the transformation of Alan into an academic as 'the goose which turned into a swan'; 'my father and I suffered successive phases of disbelief, scepticism and recognition as Alan's scholastic achievements smote us in rapid succession'; and if Alan's mother had indeed recognised his genius from the start, it didn't stop her pestering him about fingernails, hair and tidiness.

Trinity College, Cambridge, is endowed with glorious Tudor architecture. The Great Court is a place of ordered, symmetrical beauty, an open space of quietness and elegance. It was the college of Sir Isaac Newton and the place to which all aspiring mathematicians should go. Christopher Morcom had said so to Alan, and Christopher had won his scholarship to go to Trinity, so it was only natural that Alan should follow. Except that Christopher had died, and Alan's papers did not find favour with the Trinity examiners, so the name Turing went into the clearing process. Alan was handed on to King's, which was generous enough to give him a scholarship on the basis of the papers rejected by Trinity.

The architecture of King's is an untidy muddle of odd-ments thrown together over the centuries. Beginning with the absurdity of the 'chapel' – a huge medieval cathedral of unsurpassed beauty – things could only go downhill, notwith-standing desperate appeals by successive generations of college management to designers of the greatest reputation. There is an eighteenth-century wedding cake by James Gibb, seen in all calendar photos of Cambridge because it is next to the chapel, even though it doesn't belong; the third side of the Front Court is occupied by a dank Gothic nightmare by George Gilbert Scott; the range (mercifully omitted from the calendars) next to the Back Lawn is a tasting menu of early twentieth-century experiments in assorted colours and flavours. Perhaps this dis-order was well suited to someone like Alan Turing; untidiness in mathematics was to be his academic specialism and to make his reputation.

First up was the important business of becoming an undergraduate. We have little left in the record about these times. I'm delighted that he didn't do too well in his first year or so at King's: ordinary student pursuits like making friends and rowing were occupying his time. It is quite likely that, as with other students, a degree of sexual freedom came with the relative liberty of student life. It's also quite likely that there had been some preparation for this. Not for Alan the alarming tutorial which John had received; on leaving school and going to London to train as an articled clerk, Mother had been:

> prompted … to counsel me, in portentously grave tones, 'not to go off the rails'. London, she assured me, was full of temptations for young men. It was not my mother's habit to go into tedious and embarrassing detail and the temptations in question were not further specified. This was a sequel to

the famous 'birds and bees' letter some seven years earlier … handed to me by Sophie Darlington [the headmaster's wife] for private reading at Hazelhurst [John and Alan's prep school] when I was incarcerated in a room by myself with gastric flu. Sophie was brave but was on tenterhooks until she could recover the document and lock it up again.

The record does not say whether Alan also had to endure a birds-and-bees letter or off-the-rails counselling; Alan himself reckoned that a couple of terms at boarding school were sufficient to acquire some sexual experience, and the rails were pointing in a different direction at King's from London. To be precise, they were pointing to something known as the moral sciences.

Alan's first contribution to academic thought was made as an undergraduate, addressing the 'Moral Sciences Club' on 1 December 1933 under the wing of a King's fellow called R.B. Braithwaite. The title was 'Mathematics and Logic' – an overlap which you might imagine to be complete, so that there is no room for illogical mathematics. But in a university where philosophy is called 'moral sciences' there is scope for anything; Alan Turing's thesis was that it was wrong to regard mathematics as 'purely logistic' – in other words as reducible to algebraic symbols which could be processed in a formulaic way so as to spit out a black or white answer. In short, mathematics might not be wholly logical.[1]

The idea that mathematics could be fuzzy and have grey spots was a torture to the mathematicians of the early twentieth century. First the physicists had demonstrated that things at very small scale do not have sensible natural everyday behaviours – quantum mechanics is downright weird, and full of uncertainty. Alan Turing had just ploughed through John von Neumann's

Mathematische Grundlagen der Quantenmechanik – in German – and the analogy of the fundamental rules breaking down for mathematics as they had in physics would not have escaped him. Philosophical logicians like Braithwaite were less upset than the mathematicians, having recognised the difficulties of logic as applied to causes of everyday events, or to put it another way, the cussedness of things which don't work out the way you wanted.

Richard Braithwaite had been at King's since 1919, and before becoming a philosopher had been a mathematician – a wrangler (that is, with a first-class degree) at that – so was an ideal person to oversee Alan Turing's debut. To my shame, when I had the privilege of sitting next to Braithwaite at a King's College dinner in 1980, as an undergraduate, I had no idea who he was, or how influential he had been in my uncle's intellectual development, as one of the body who elected Alan to a fellowship. Nor that he had been one of the two dons, both from King's, who had put forward the official proposal in 1946 which, at last, allowed Cambridge women to be awarded degrees. So the conversation was just regular college small talk, and I came away with the impression that Braithwaite was just another one of the elderly and friendly philosophy dons of which King's seemed to have dozens. A missed opportunity, which I much regret.

Alan Turing had just made headlines. 'Caught up in Cambridge's climate of treason,' blazed a *Guardian* headline on Monday, 14 January 1980, juxtaposing it with a piece about Anthony Blunt, one of the notorious Cambridge spy ring who had just been stripped of his knighthood. An over-enthusiastic sub-editor had pieced together the sensational idea that, because Alan Turing was at Cambridge at the same time as Blunt, Philby and Burgess; was gay; and worked indirectly for the Secret Intelligence Service, he therefore was associated with the Cambridge spies. It was a journalistic syllogism, if not a meticulous exercise in logic. There were only a few things wrong with it (the spies were at Trinity, which had rejected Alan; Bletchley Park was not the same thing as MI6; oh, and the minor inconvenience that Alan Turing had not spied for the Soviet Union), but who was going to let facts get in the way of a nice headline?

While Alan was at King's College himself, he had indeed dipped his toe into political waters. In 1933, he disliked the film *Our Fighting Navy*, considering it 'blatant militarist propaganda'; and on a holiday to Germany in 1934, he chided his friend Denis Williams for saying '*Heil Hitler*' (seemingly nothing more than polite usage in those early days of Nazism). That was it, for Alan's involvement in politics; alas for *The Guardian*, not a communist in sight.

This effort at fake news (for which *The Guardian* graciously apologised a few days later) marks the starting point for Alan Turing becoming famous for the second time – it was supposed to be a pre-publicity effort for Andrew Hodges's comprehensive biography of a previously unknown mathematician who had had a pivotal role in codebreaking during World War Two.[2] Alan was not around to deal with the fame, this time; brother John, who was still alive, together with eight members of the great and good (including some from Bletchley and King's, and Andrew Hodges himself) were left to write the required letter of dismay. While this was going on, I was eating profiteroles with Professor Braithwaite, learning to row, and – avoiding all exposure to moral sciences – wholly oblivious that Alan Turing's second round of fame would be shaped as much by the media as by fact.

My own decision to go to King's College, Cambridge, was deliberate: if Alan had gone there then that was the target, the role to follow. There was a certain amount of negotiation about it, with my housemaster at Sherborne, who didn't know anyone at King's and so felt unable to get me in by his efforts. Actually, I wanted to get in through my own efforts rather than string-pulling, and I wonder still whether the reputation that King's had for being rather left wing had something to do with his reluctance (his idea was that I should go to Corpus, which he described as a 'very public school sort of college' – no words could have been better chosen to ensure that I stubbornly stuck to my own choice). And I suppose it was, partly, Alan's legacy that I chose to study science subjects there, though subsequently I realised that my skills are not best used in that field. By the time I got to King's, via some flaw in the left-wing arrangements, the news that Alan Turing had been gay was out, and so were the first hints of what had been done at Bletchley. But still the name of Turing was hardly known, and there was a certain amount of good-natured teasing at King's when fellows of the college asked me within earshot of other students whether I was related to 'the great Turing'.

These days, King's rates Alan Turing among its most famous alumni. John Maynard Keynes, Rupert Brooke, Xu Zhimo and Sir Robert Walpole are some of the others, indicating that not much fame happened between 1698 (when Walpole left) and 1901 (when Keynes arrived). The poet Xu is hardly known outside China but the small stone memorial among the daffodils by the bridge over the Cam is a place of pilgrimage for visitors to the college. Keynes has the doubtful honour of a 1960s building – one of King's experiments in incongruous architecture – to commemorate him; the ongoing third round of fame associated with Alan Turing has suggested to the college that a sculpture by Sir Antony Gormley (an alumnus of Trinity College) would be an idea – an idea reportedly causing dismay

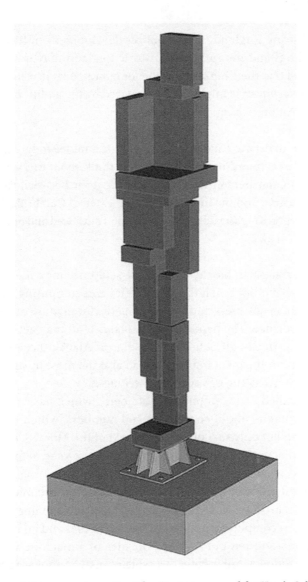

The sculpture commemorating Alan Turing proposed for King's College.
(Antony Gormley Studio/Cambridge City Council)

to Historic England, which polices development in historic buildings and monuments. Historic England may not have noticed that the King's reputation for monuments in a consistently elegant style might not be damaged by the addition.

Sir Antony was quoted as saying:

> I am in debt to King's College and its committee for giving me an extraordinary opportunity to think about this very particular person who unlocked the door between the industrial and the information ages … Of all Cambridge's colleges, King's has always been the most advanced and open to the new.

The rectangular, blocky style of the sculpture may stand for the 'logistic' approach to mathematics and computing, Alan Turing's major pre-war discovery and the foundation of computer science. The paper which explains it all may get fewer citations in Google Scholar than some of Alan's other works, but is both the most important, and also the most misunderstood, of Alan Turing's academic writings.

It's called 'On Computable Numbers',[3] which has come to mean that it's about computing and numbers, which is sort of right, but only sort of. In the context of the Moral Sciences Club discussion which took place about a year before he started working on the paper, it's actually about logic and the limitations of what can be proved using a mechanical, or robotic, process. Alan Turing invited his readers to imagine a (human) computer equipped with a set of rules and no imagination, and then put forward the idea of a machine which could follow similar rules – a table of instructions – in like fashion. The machine would get its input by reading symbols printed on a tape, and produce its output by writing symbols onto the tape. This type of machine, able only to do what it is told in the instruction table, has limitations, but the idea of the 'universal' machine which can process any set of instructions that you give it has profoundly interesting implications in mathematical logic. The mindless machine (or, to be more exact, the machine and the instruction tables) described by Alan is now known as a Turing machine, and it's what made him famous the first time.

But robotically following instructions is not the only way to proceed, as anyone who had tried to control a room full of human computers in the 1930s well knew. In a later paper called 'Systems of Logic based on Ordinals', Alan introduced the idea of an 'oracle' machine which could do things that the Turing machine could not – in essence, a machine which could introduce some degree of arbitrariness into the computation process. [4] 'Systems of Logic' (described by Alan's best friend Robin Gandy as 'a stinker to read') introduced the concept of intuition into mathematics. Those who wanted mathematics and logic and proof to follow along tramlines must have been horrified by oracles and intuition. Great mathematics has always been able to see through fog: finding proofs is rarely about following the rulebook. We still struggle with the notion that computers, or artificial intelligence, might do things smacking of imagination, intuition or creativity, partly because we are stuck with a perception of what computers can and cannot do ('they just do what they are programmed to do'), all because the paper which created computer science apparently put boundaries around it.

There's only one problem with all this – 'On Computable Numbers' and 'Systems of Logic' are all about potential, not limitations. 'On Computable Numbers' doesn't define upper limits on what machines might do, and Alan Turing comes back to this in later writings. To say that a human mind can't possibly be emulated by a machine is to confuse the limitations of a Turing-machine algorithm – a mindless, robotic procedure, as described in 'On Computable Numbers' – with a much bigger thing, comprising both machine and software. Limitations are inherent in the mechanistic approach to programming – the routine following of a sequence of instructions, which themselves are limited in scope – and exploring the implications of such limits was an interesting question in number theory, but never an analysis of what computing machinery could do in real life. Our world just isn't digital, however much we are in thrall to our smartphones and laptops, and Alan Turing was all too aware of that. We can, and do, achieve all sorts of interesting things, and as he proved, some of it just doesn't compute. Computing, in the sense of the Turing machine, is programming, and not everything is a program.

By the early 1950s, when digital stored-program computers were a reality and abuzz in the media, the Turing machine had acquired a mythology all of its own:

> *Türing Machine.* In 1936 Dr Turing wrote a paper on the design and the limitations of computing machines. For this reason they are sometimes known by his name. The umlaut is an unearned and undesirable addition, due, presumably, to an impression that anything so incomprehensible must be Teutonic.[5]

(Well, it does look a bit German, and I have myself been given the occasional umlaut, even when I thought I was making myself perfectly clear. Actually, the name is Scottish, originally spelt 'Turyn', when King Robert Bruce granted fishing rights to an ancestor of mine near a golf course belonging to Donald Trump. Trump came along a bit later. I don't own the fishing rights, and so have had no occasion to tangle lines with the 45th President of the United States.) The umlauted quote comes from a book called *Faster than Thought*, published in 1953 and reprinted four times over the next ten years, which was a popular-science explanation of everything you could then want to know about computers. I suspect that the unearned umlaut came from one of those uncomputed associations of ideas: the Turing machine concept was used by Alan to answer the 'Decidability Question' (about the provability of theorems); it followed in the footsteps of the Austrian mathematician Kurt Gödel, who had answered the 'Completeness Question' (about the existence of unproveable theorems). Clearly, a follower of Gödel ought to have an umlaut, even if it's no more Scottish than Mr Trump. As to *Faster than Thought*, Alan Turing said it was 'a little book which Ferranti's are getting out to boost their machine',[6] but when he made this catty remark he was referring deprecatingly to a piece he had contributed on chess-playing programs, and it was said to fend off a piece of fake news about a reported, but imaginary, chess match between the Ferranti computer at Manchester and another machine in Princeton:

> The Manchester machine has 3,500 tubes, 12 c-r [cath-ode ray] storage tubes, 100,000 soldered joints, 6 miles of wire and a power consumption of 27 kilowatts. It can also be beaten, regularly, by any human chess player in the master class, many of whom live largely on corn flakes, cor-responding to not more than 100 watts, with no soldered connections whatever.[7]

Without the need for cornflakes, or even an umlaut, the Manchester computer which was being boosted in *Faster than Thought* was quite capable of misbehaviour. Early computers were temperamental, as Alan Turing himself noted in a broadcast in January 1952:

> Computing machines aren't really infallible at all. Making up checks on their accuracy is quite an important part of the art of using them. Besides making mistakes they sometimes haven't done quite the calculation one had expected, and one gets something that might be called a 'misunderstanding'.[8]

The wobbly technology of the late 1940s made running a successful routine some way off the pure algorithmic ideal of the Turing machine.

The concept of the Turing machine, and the role that Alan Turing had played along the way in showing the holes in mathematical logic, had already made him slightly famous.

The challenges of programming in 1953: Alan Turing's note shows that the machine has misbehaved. (Reproduced by kind permission of the University of Manchester)

Mathematicians and logicians recognised the unusual name, even without the umlaut. For Alan, this may have been gratifying – he indicates as much in his single foray into fiction (it's terrible, and mercifully he gave up after a handful of badly scribbled and crossed-out pages)[9] – but equally it could be tedious to be stalked by fans of the Turing machine. On one occasion in 1952, 'Alan suddenly disappeared through one doorway on spotting a particularly dull logician bear down upon him from another'.[10]

By 1952, Alan's fame had notched up slightly; the reason he was on the wireless, talking about the fallibility of computing machines, was that he was caught up in a tiny storm over the troublesome topic of computers muscling in on the human preserve. Specifically, a vexed and emotive question about the definition of humanity, presented to the world as a question about whether a machine could be said to 'think'. The media called the thing the 'electronic brain', and the idea was sufficiently creepy to merit a short run of talks on the *Third Programme* (now BBC Radio Three), somewhat in the style of the more recent *Horizon* series on BBC2, starring the mysterious Dr Turing.

Fame because you had been on the wireless was different from fame in the rarefied field of logic, because friends and family were involved; it was a tame sort of fame nonetheless, since the *Third Programme* was not really mass-media popular entertainment. Still, it was a certainty that Mother was listening. Even Alan himself had to listen: 'I listened to broadcast,' he wrote to Mother. 'It was rather better than I had expected, and I found my voice rather less trying to listen to than before.'[11]

That comment is a footnote at the end of a letter which raises more questions than one might imagine. The purpose of it was to agree to Mother's suggestion that she no longer needed the £50 a month allowance Alan had been paying her since 1949. Aunt Sibyl, Julius Turing's sister, had died leaving Alan's mother £5,000, and Alan's advice had been sought on how to deal with the bequest. Sara Turing (as she now was) had been widowed in 1947, after a period of separation from Julius, so the gift from Sibyl to Sara as estranged sister-in-law was doubly generous. Even more bizarre is the idea of Sara taking financial advice from Alan, when Sara's other son, John – whose professional life was almost entirely spent in giving advice to the wealthy on management of their affairs – lived right next door. One is tempted to imagine that John did not know of the £50 a month, and to conclude that Alan and John were not really communicating. The letter is dated 19 January 1952. Less than three weeks later, Alan was arrested. John's help, as brother and solicitor, was invoked, but John found the subject of homosexuality unpleasant, if not downright disgusting, and, because it involved his brother, humiliating and shameful. The help was forthcoming but tainted by such feelings, and John's shock – he had no idea that Alan was gay until he read the fateful letter announcing the arrest – clouded their relationship still further.

The kind of fame which came with being on the wireless was, owing to the arrest, in danger of becoming a kind of notoriety instead. The papers, naturally, liked the idea of one of the elite being brought down. The hearings were in open court with reporters present, though the tameness of *Third Programme* fame meant that the distance Alan could fall was rather limited. In the circumstances, the media coverage was not too bad; only the local papers were interested, and prosecutions for homosexual behaviour were not much of a novelty in 1952. John's fears were probably overimagined and, perversely, a reflection of his own pride in his brother's small-scale fame.

By 1952, the Turing machine was no longer a novel concept in mathematics, even if it was being embodied in the electronic brains described in *Faster than Thought*. When the book was issued in January 1953, Alan Turing had disengaged from computer design and mathematical logic. But not from mathematics: his new work on morphogenesis was entirely about the mathematical modelling of chemical diffusion, as a possible explanation of shapes and patterns in living things. He was using the computer to grind through the calculations implied by his equations; and also to pick up another loose thread in number theory which he had also explored, with an idea for a machine, in the pre-war years.

One influence on Alan Turing, while he was still a student at Cambridge, was the mathematician A.E. Ingham. In his spare time from teaching Alan, Ingham was working on a study of the distribution of prime numbers, published in 1934. If computable numbers cause confusion, prime numbers are a bit easier to grasp; nevertheless, they are a rum bunch, because they aren't spaced out according to any obvious pattern. 1, 2, 3, 5, 7, 11 – it looks as if they're getting further apart, but later on you get 29 and 31 which are too close for comfort, and this kind of thing goes on right along the series. Ingham's book devotes much of itself to speculations by the nineteenth-century mathematician Riemann, which included the idea that the distribution of 'zeroes' of his zeta function might be similar to the distribution of prime numbers.

Alan Turing was obviously fascinated by the Riemann problem. The only thing standing in the way of testing Riemann's hypothesis was calculating the values of the zeta function. Even Alan admitted that 'the most laborious part of such calculations consists in the evaluation of certain trigonometric sums'. Fortunately, the approximation was very like a formula already being used to compute tidal motion – and there was a machine doing just that, in Liverpool. Invented by Lord Kelvin in 1872, this was an analogue computer which measured the effect of various things pulling the tide this way and that, and their interplay with each other, through a series of pulleys and rotating discs which implemented the cosine function. All Alan Turing had to do was build a similar machine, then he could compute the zeros of the Riemann zeta function and solve the prime number distribution problem! He put in a grant proposal in 1939, asking for £40, from which the quote above was taken.[12]

With or without the grant, work was started, and brass gear-wheels were famously strewn over the floor of his rooms in King's College – but the Riemann machine was never finished. The work was interrupted by politics. What's interesting is that Alan Turing, the person who defined the theory of a digital computer in his 'On Computable Numbers' paper, had turned

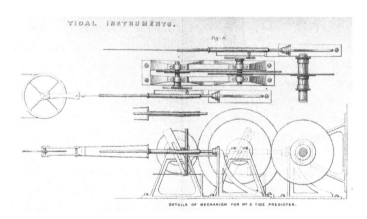

Lord Kelvin's 'tide predicter' (*sic*). (*Minutes of the Proceedings of the Institute of Civil Engineers*, 1881)

to an analogue solution to do the computations. In 1939, the £40 grant would be a far cheaper way to do it than hiring a small army of human computers. What hadn't occurred to Alan Turing, apparently, was to solve the problem with a digital computer. Not yet, though the political interruption would alter his thinking on that score.

By the time Alan Turing got back to work on the Riemann question after the war, he did have an electronic computer to work with, and published his results in 1953 in the *Proceedings of the London Mathematical Society*.[13] 'If it had not been for the fact that the computer remained in serviceable condition for an unusually long period from 3 p.m. one afternoon to 8 a.m. the following morning it is probable that the calculations would never have been done at all.' Even technology faster than thought left a daunting problem, and Alan's partial solution says little about prime numbers.

In the meantime, politics had inducted Alan Turing into a completely new profession, one which, in 1938, was firmly embedded in the use of squared paper and pencils for solving its problems. Following a set of routine instructions with squared paper and pencils was what human computers did. Following a set of instructions to write and erase digits onto squares on strips of paper was also what Turing machines did. Codebreaking was a digital world, with the disruptions of intuition and imagination thrown in to make it interesting.

Codebreaking nowadays is theoretically indebted to Alan Turing's 1936 thinking on computability. It's not just that computers became a powerful force at the disposal of the codebreakers in the post-war years, but that the battle between codemakers and codebreakers fundamentally depends on computability. For Alan Turing's papers setting out the theory of computation led directly to the idea that some problems are easier to solve, taking less time and electricity, than others: the notion of relative computability. What the codemakers want is something which is easy to verify, once the solution is known, but incredibly hard to find when the solution is not known. One simple example of such a problem is the 'integer partition problem', but plenty of others exist.

Alan Turing at about the time of writing his paper *On Computable Numbers*. (Reproduced by kind permission of the Provost and Scholars of King's College, Cambridge)

The integer partition problem – an example

Can you package up the following numbers into three groups which have equal totals?

19, 20, 22, 23, 25, 27, 40, 45, 49

Yes: each of these groups [19, 22, 49], [20, 25, 45] and [23, 27, 40] adds up to 90. Easy to check, but is there a neat algorithm to sort the numbers into those groups, other than by brute force (trial and error)?

Unawares, we're dependent on these asymmetric things – easy-to-verify, hard-to-solve structures with relatively hard computability – to keep our credit card data safe, since the encryption systems we use to send information securely rely on it being much too time-consuming to try to discover the secret information by hacking, while a legitimate recipient can use a key to unlock it speedily. Unless, of course, you're a Bitcoin miner, rewarded for 'mining' (which is a cute name for code-cracking), or you were dumb enough to set your password as 12345.

In early 1939, while Alan Turing was assembling small brass gears for his Riemann machine and Adolf Hitler was assembling small bits of Europe for darker purposes, the question was whether the process of computing could be done fast enough to break into the most secure encryption mechanism of the day. Enigma was not going to be broken by brute force, even with squared paper and female computers. Something new was needed, and it might just be something like a Turing machine.

GEHEIM

The Enigma. Codebreaker. Alan Turing Decoded. Breaking the Code. The Enigma Man. And so on. Books and plays and screenplays about Alan Turing home in on codebreaking. But World War Two was an interlude in his academic career – a period which, in the opinion of some mathematicians discussing Alan's career in 1970, were the 'wasted years'.[1] Why is Alan Turing now known as a brilliant codebreaker, whereas in the period before 1980 he was known, if at all, as the pioneer of computer science?

Of course, the answer is bound up in the success of the British Establishment in keeping the secret of Bletchley Park just that, a secret, for a full thirty years after the end of World War Two. But surely that is not the complete answer – unless it's true that Alan Turing's skills as a codebreaker surpassed everything else he did. Perhaps we need to take a look at Alan's new-found reputation as 'the codebreaker who saved millions of lives', as the BBC described him in 2012, the centenary year of his birth.[2] I strongly suspect that Alan Turing had not the faintest idea that such a thing would ever be said of him, and if he were to have heard it in his lifetime he would, without false modesty, have denied that anything so foolish could have been asserted.

If I am going to upset the many thousands of Alan Turing hero-worshippers with such an outrageous statement, I suppose I ought to explain myself. Bletchley Park was, undoubtedly, a place where amazing things were done which had an immensely significant influence on the course of the war. The official historian of British Intelligence in the Second World War, Sir F.H. Hinsley, said that without the work of Bletchley Park, 'the war would have been something like two years longer, perhaps three years longer, possibly four';[3] he was there, and I am not going to quarrel with that. But there is a leap from saying that to saying that Alan Turing saved millions of lives. Somehow, the stories of Bletchley, Enigma and Alan have become conflated into a single heroic narrative. Perhaps the stepping stones are that Alan Turing cracked the 'unbreakable' Enigma problem, and that Enigma was the most significant success story of Bletchley Park.

I don't know why Enigma is the star of the show. The present Bletchley Park research historian, Dr David Kenyon, has commented on how difficult it can be to work out which bits of intelligence derived from Enigma decrypts or from other sources.[4] Of course, there are numerous well-documented examples where it was specifically Enigma that made a real difference (the U-boat war, the Battle of Matapan, the 'battle of the beams' during the Blitz, and so on). For historians, though, the difficulty is that by the second half of the war, Bletchley was getting its material from a vast range of sources, and like a good intelligence organisation, brought together everything it knew from all sources to present an overall appreciation to its military clients. Besides Enigma, there were innumerable hand-ciphers, Japanese ciphers, and the Lorenz teleprinter traffic, mostly deciphered by hand but famously also using the Colossus machine and its predecessors (oh dear, there are still those who think that Colossus was used to break Enigma, and 1945 photos of Colossus routinely feature as illustrations to newspaper articles on Enigma – a measure of how much Enigma has stolen the limelight). All these contributed to the signals intelligence picture, in proportions we still do not understand.

But Enigma is the prima donna. Maybe understanding its complexity is just about within reach of most of us: we can grasp its workings and be awestruck by the difficulty of the problem. The teleprinter cipher machine is a step too far, so we'd prefer to focus on Enigma. It's also true that Enigma was a prodigious source of material (even though much of it could be as unexciting as '*Keine Zusätze zum Vorbericht*' – nothing to add to report). But maybe it's because it was the first success against a machine cipher, because it was (possibly) the first time machines were used in codebreaking, and because Alan Turing was at the centre of that work.

Alan Turing first stepped down into the underworld of the cryptanalysts in 1938, when he was approached by Alastair Denniston, then the head of the Government Code & Cypher School, as a potential recruit for his reserve list of 'men of the professor type'. Acting on instructions from his boss in MI6, Denniston was looking out for mathematicians, since MI6 thought they might do better against machine ciphers such as Enigma than the linguists that the GC&CS typically had on its books. Alan Turing was a match, largely because he was a fellow of King's College, Cambridge, which is what passed for a recruitment profile in 1938. No codebreaking aptitude was called for, and if any evidence for that is needed you need look no further than some of the other King's fellows who were hired: F.L. Lucas (English literature); Christopher Morris (history); Patrick Wilkinson (classics); Alexis Vlasto (Russian); Philip Hall (mathematics) – to name just a handful.[5] All these men contributed greatly to the successes of Bletchley Park, and none of them was remotely involved in the Enigma problem. On the other hand, the greatest of the Enigma codebreakers, Dilly Knox, was a fellow of King's too, whose codebreaking achievements began in the previous war, and that explains a lot about the recruitment policy. Following his recruitment, Alan Turing was sent on a codebreaking course in January 1939, and assigned to work with Knox on the Enigma challenge.

So, of course, with Alan Turing on the case, it was a short step from there to the invention of the famous Bombe machine which was in production by early 1940, and producing its priceless results by the time of the Battle of Britain, which we won, and because we held off the German invasion in 1940 one thing led to another, and we won the whole war. Except that obviously this comic-book account is too trite. So what actually happened?

The problem facing the British in 1939 was that they didn't know how the German military version of the Enigma machine was wired up internally, and in particular they didn't know how the plugboard on the front of the machine fitted into the encryption mechanism. The information about this was gifted to Denniston and Knox at a meeting in Warsaw in the last week of July 1939; actually, that makes it even more remarkable that the Bombe machine design was in the hands of engineers by the end of autumn of the same year. But it wasn't a miracle or even the unimaginable stubborn genius of Alan Turing working on his own in a shed (as you might think, if you have seen the movie *The Imitation Game*) which allowed such an astonishing advance in only four months. The fact is that the Polish codebreakers who had reverse-engineered the German military Enigma had invented their own mechanical methods for breaking Enigma, and they had included all the details in the Warsaw briefing. The Polish work had started in earnest in 1933, and the British had been saved six years' work in the course of a meeting lasting just two days.

One of the devices explained to Knox and Denniston was a thing called a *bomba*. No one knows for sure why it was called that, though there are several fun theories, most of which have to do with ice cream and none of which have anything to do with breaking German ciphers. The *bomba* was a brute-force device which clanked sequentially through all 17,576 possible positions in which the three coding wheels of the Enigma machine could be as it enciphered a message. If you were lucky, one of those positions was the one from which the Germans had begun encipherment. You needed luck, because you still had to guess which wheels had been selected, the order in which they had been put into the machine, what the plugboard cross-wirings were, and the positions of the 'tyres' which can be slid around the outside of each wheel to disguise the orientation of the wheel's wiring. But what was clever about the *bomba* was its logic.

Logic was something in which Alan Turing specialised, in particular the kind of mathematical logic implied in mechanical processing. The *bomba*'s logic was – like a Turing machine embodied in physical form – that it would stop when it found a plausible starting position for the three wheels; and to know whether to stop, it needed to test something. The Poles had exploited a feature of German radio signals procedure which involved repeating part of the preamble, so that a sequence of three letters (say, A-B-C) got enciphered twice (giving, say,

V-R-B-N-Q-A). Sometimes a repetition came up in the enciphered sequence (like B-K-W-B-D-Y); and the *bomba*'s job
was to detect wheel positions which would allow this type of
repeat. Alan Turing was given all this information on a plate
at the end of July 1939, as soon as Knox got back from Poland.

So, when Alan Turing turned up for work at Bletchley at
the outbreak of war, he was already working on a design for a
souped-up British version of the *bomba*. Documents in the UK
National Archives show that Alan, together with Knox and three
others, wanted to have at least one *bomba* similar to the Polish
design,[6] but it was foolish to bet everything on the continua-
tion by the Germans of the repeated preamble. The professional
codebreakers (on both sides) tut-tutted about the preamble – the
British thought the Germans would change the procedure, and
sure enough the Germans did, just as they invaded France in
May 1940. The British Enigma-cracking machine needed to be
better than the *bomba* but it could still exploit its fundamental
features: brute-force testing of all 17,576 wheel positions and
stopping at a plausible candidate for the one the Germans had
actually used. With all respect to Alan Turing, he did not invent
these features of the British war-winning weapon we know as
the Bombe. As the cryptanalytical historians C.A. Deavours and
Louis Kruh say, 'Turing claimed that his original idea for the
bombe design came from Polish work.'[7]

He was being modest, for what he did do was nevertheless
hugely imaginative, and converted an interesting prototype
idea (the *bomba*) into something much more powerful. The
first task was to move to a new logical test, if the duplicated
preamble wasn't going to remain in effect. At this point, Alan
Turing's partnership with Dilly Knox bore fruit. As a veteran
codebreaker of the old school, Knox used the 'probable word
attack' in his own codebreaking work: this is when you guess

at some part of the content of the enciphered message, and try to match up the cipher-text with the guessed clear text. Both of them knew that the Enigma could not encipher any letter as itself, so that gave a tiny way into lining up a guessed-at probable word against the cipher-text: if a message contains the word LUFTWAFFE, it might be that the sequence of letters GXVVUFSRZ found in the cipher-text match up to LUFTWAFFE, but the sequence VUFSRZQME could not (because U, F and E cannot encipher as themselves). Marrying Knox's probable words with the Polish stopping-system was the new logic.

Much more inventive, impressive, time-saving and unimaginable was Alan Turing's addition to the test. The chunter through 17,576 wheel positions sounds like it saves a lot of work, but the biggest mathematical challenge of the Enigma machine was the plugboard – the feature the British had not got to grips with before July 1939 – which has 150,738,274,937,250 different possible set-ups if the Germans used ten cross-connections. Alan Turing's main contribution to the design of the Bombe was to crack open the plugboard. The plugboard was the feature which gave the security staff of the German Armed Forces High Command (OKW) the confidence that Enigma messages would stay *geheim* (secret). The OKW were fully aware that machinery could be deployed against Enigma – indeed, they were using punched-card machines to attack Allied codes themselves – but a process to find one straw in a stack of 150,738,274,937,250 was, they thought, beyond reach. Wrong: Alan Turing found a way, in 1939, to reveal the cross-pluggings, and to do it semi-automatically. Sets of replica Enigma wheels were connected up for the probable word test using 26-wire cables, one wire for each letter of the alphabet, and voltage would be applied to just one test wire. The test wire would indicate a possible plugboard connection, and each letter in the probable word could be checked, using another machine called, imaginatively enough, a checking machine, to find further connections. The extra addition to the Polish technology was what made the Bombe so powerful and valuable; oddly, as an engineering feature, it's a tiny inconspicuous little thing on the side of the Bombe machine which you would miss unless the demonstrator at the National Museum of Computing points it out to you.

If you watch the film *The Imitation Game*, you could be forgiven for thinking that the struggle to produce the Bombe machine took place in the face of official opposition, lack of confidence from colleagues, and as a result of sweated labour lasting not just months but years. Fortunately, Hollywood does not have to stick to what is found in the archives, so the moviegoers can get a great sense of the challenges facing Bletchley even if a certain liberty is taken with the chronology and characters. That's a theme to come back to; the point for the present is that there was official support for building the Bombe, not just from Denniston, but significantly from his energetic and forceful deputy, Commander Edward Travis, and Alan's ideas benefited from the support, technical input and interpretation skills of the small Enigma research team at Bletchley. Notably, Peter Twinn, the first mathematician hired by GC&CS ever (in 1939), helped the engineers translate the Turing ideas from concept to blueprints to relays and cams, and Gordon Welchman, another mathematician from Cambridge, added his own design feature called the 'diagonal board' which reduced the number of false stops (incorrect solutions) of the Bombe, converting it into something practically useable for the duration of the war. The engineers who brought this oddity into existence had to do more than just turn wiring diagrams into a box with wheels on it: the plugboard test required that the machine stop when it *failed* to detect electric current running through any wire in the 26-wire cabling, which was an innovation in relay-based switching technology in the 1930s. To get the Bombe into an effective working state by the time Britain was under serious threat in the late summer of 1940 was an astonishing achievement, and it was a team effort. Undoubtedly, Alan Turing's vision for solving the plugboard was the greatest and most inventive element, but he would have denied that the whole thing was a creature of his making.

What convinces me that he was so dependent on the Polish leg-up is not just the decision to call the British Enigma-breaking machine the Bombe, in honour of their preceding work, nor the copying of the attack on the three coding wheels, but the difference of approach from the analogue machine which Alan Turing had been building only months before in order to tackle his Riemann zeta function problem. The Bombe is basically a digital machine, turning the manufacturer's expertise in punched-card machine computing in a new direction. Although some of its 'logic' is hard-wired, it's partly programmable, like the Hollerith machines the manufacturers regularly built, and it's a step on the road away from single-purpose analogue computing machines and heading slowly towards modern digital computers. Alan Turing may have learned as much from the Bombe's engineering design as he contributed to its logic. The digital approach of using Hollerith punched-card machines to assist with codebreaking was adopted by the British, and the Germans, in their respective cryptanalytical efforts; to me it is a wonder that the elegant and sophisticated algorithms used by both sides in their Hollerith units to save time and winnow out codebreaking solutions attract so little interest. Perhaps they, too, were influential in the way post-war computing developed.

If the Bombe's design – the main solution to the Enigma problem – was basically done before the war began in earnest for the British in 1940, there is a rather big question about what Alan Turing was actually doing during the fighting years. To begin with, there was the challenge of Naval Enigma. The German Navy did things differently from their Army and Air Force, and the method of encryption was far more secure. One difference was in the preamble to the message, which contained vital clues to the set-up of their Enigma machines. Alan Turing apparently discovered the methodology in late 1939,[8] but knowing the method is not the same as decrypting intercepted messages – the method used secret tables of bigrams, combinations of two letters, distributed to ships and U-boats. At the same time as uncovering the bigram method, Alan had created a codebreaking technique later called 'Banburismus', named after the nursery-rhyme town Banbury, where long sheets of paper were printed with the alphabet for use with the technique. Banburismus was a method for finding which coding wheel was in the rightmost position in the Enigma machine.

Except that Alan Turing's Banburismus wasn't really Alan Turing's idea at all – apart from the long sheets of paper, it was the Polish 'clock method' described to Knox and Denniston at the meeting five months before,[9] so the emergence of Banburismus together with the discovery of the preamble method was in fact one discovery, rather than two. In any case, Banburismus itself wasn't much use until 1941, when a set of the secret bigram tables was captured in Norway. It actually doesn't matter who discovered what, but that the Banburismus technique was an example of a more rigorous, mathematical approach to probability being introduced into British cryptanalysis. Alan Turing instigated it: the reintroduction of Bayesian probability methods into mainstream thinking. Start with a hypothesis; use the evidence, however small, to modify it and improve the hypothesis. The method worked for things like deciding which coding wheel was in the rightmost position in the German U-boats' Enigma machines, using Banburismus to weed out less probable candidates. Because it was Bletchley, probability had to have its own arcane vocabulary; measures of likelihood invented by Alan Turing were the 'ban' and the 'deciban' – also derivatives of Banbury. The town has more to things to be proud of than cakes and a cross.

The capture of the German naval bigram tables was a military operation, a raid in which men lost their lives. Bletchley Park presents a glamorised picture of the war, in which doughty folk worked with pencils as weapons and whose sufferings were to endure the winter cold in unheated smoke-filled dingy huts. War is not like that, though it suits us to celebrate the sanitised and intellectualised side of it. It is brutalising and disgusting, and a licence for people to do revolting things. Bletchley Park's job was to abet those things, but its people avoided the worst of it. They knew it, too, because their friends and families had no such way out. The families, of course, wanted to know what military-age folk were doing if they were not in uniform (the social pressure explains why younger recruits to Bletchley in the middle and latter stages of the war were – if men – given wartime commissions into one of the armed services; women at Bletchley weren't all WRNS, WAAFs or ATS, since presumably the pressures were different). Some felt this pressure keenly, though for Alan Turing's family it was clear he was doing something important and highly secret, and that this was a far better idea than sending him off with a rifle to fight the Germans face to face.

Alongside almost all of Bletchley's staff, Alan tried to keep the details of how he was occupied a secret from outsiders, including from his brother John and from Mother. In her biography of Alan, first published in 1959, Sara wrote coyly that:

> he was taken on as a temporary Civil Servant in the Foreign Office, in the Department of Communications ... At first even his whereabouts were kept secret, but later it was divulged that he was working at Bletchley Park, Bletchley. No hint was ever given of the nature of his secret work, nor has it ever been revealed.

This made for a short chapter, which concerns itself with Alan's failings as a correspondent and his eccentricities as a co-worker. But the Turings, while not in on the secret, could piece things together. It wasn't the mathematical approach to probability measured by bans and decibans, but it did allow for deductions. John learned, in 1944, that his superior officer Colonel Pat Webster also had a brother working in an obscure town called Bletchley; they speculated that their brothers' work must have to do with codes and ciphers – the 'Department of Communications' would otherwise be too unlikely by half a ban or more.

John (my father) had joined the Territorial Army before the war, on the principle that it was better to join voluntarily rather than be pressed when the inevitable happened. This meant that he found himself an officer, of the lowest possible commissioned rank, when it did; while Alan was wrestling with the under-performing prototype Bombe at Bletchley, John was trying to fend off the German Blitzkrieg in France with feeble weapons as well:

We arrive at so-called defensive posns and find that A Coy
have put our road-block in a differen posn. I get Sgt Stocker
to cut down a tree to fortify it … I suppose we had been up
on the road about 15 mins when tracer bullets come crack-
ing down the road from the Amiens direction – ack, ack,
ack, ack, ack – and large pieces of road-block, branches of
trees and what-have-you started falling all around … I could
see my men keeping well into the ditch and told them to
get their packs off + leave them behind wherever we might
go. They were as scared as hell and so was I … An enemy
AFV [tank] comes up and pots at us from about 300x with
tracer-bullets and sets some of the haycocks on fire. Most of
the shots go high but others whip through the grass. Teddy
and I shout ourselves hoarse telling the men to keep down
and fire at it whilst others withdraw. It has some effect. At
any rate the tank stops. If only it knew that we have no A-Tk
[anti-tank] rifle + it could come up and enfilade us! I have
no hope whatever of getting out of this jam. We seem to be
sheep for the slaughter.

That comes from John's handwritten war diary, kept contrary
to the King's Regulations. It was 20 May 1940, a month before
the final French surrender on 22 June. Somehow, 2/Lieut
J.F. Turing, B Coy, 2/5th Bn Queen's Royal Regt, made it across
to Cherbourg and back to England. There, at Bletchley Park,
the crucial addition to the Bombe was suggested by Alan's
colleague Gordon Welchman, and the turbo-charged version
was installed in August the same year. It was just in time:
German attacks on Britain began in earnest in the late summer
of 1940, and the Blitzkrieg became, for British people suffering
air raids, the Blitz.

The first twelve months of World War Two mark the high point of Alan Turing's inventiveness in cryptanalysis, even though the problems did not disappear with the commissioning of a fully effective Bombe. Enigma represented a continually evolving problem, as the German forces adapted their machines and their signalling techniques. It was a constant game of catch-up; all the while, though, Bletchley Park was becoming more mechanised, cryptanalytical processes were becoming standardised, and new people were coming in as the GC&CS grew. New types of codes and ciphers needed to be tackled, and Germany was not the only foreign power of concern. The skills required were concentration, attention to detail and accuracy, with, ideally, a seasoning of psychological insight into the enemy's mind. Not all of these characteristics are commonly associated with Alan Turing. By 1942, when there were nearly fifty Bombe machines pitted against Enigma[10] in a factory-like process, there were fewer of the analytical problems which best suited the common-room approach of the older codebreakers (such as Alan Turing, who at 30 years old was almost a veteran) and much, much more management. Bletchley Park was evolving from a pre-war dinosaur into a modern organisation which needed to be run on industrial lines, and it was far from clear how Alan would fit in.

On 1 February 1942, as Bletchley was beginning the painful process of shedding its ill-fitting pre-war skin, the German Navy brought into service a fourth wheel for U-boat Enigma machine communications. It was not a surprise to the Allies, who had been told (by the Germans, in encrypted messages, which they had intercepted and decrypted) about the change well in advance; nevertheless, the technology was lagging on the Allied side. Late in 1942, the British still had not developed a satisfactory four-wheel Bombe, and the Americans had lost patience, as well as shipping. Secondments can be a useful way to manage staff questions in a modern business, and in the spirit of modernity Alan Turing was sent off to the United States to act as a consultant to the American Navy team, who were dealing with the four-wheel Enigma problem for themselves.

It was the time that the 'hinge of fate', in Churchill's phrase, was turning. In October 1942, the first meaningful victory was obtained against Axis forces in North Africa with Montgomery's El Alamein offensive. In November, the Americans landed in the west, and the process of expunging the Axis from the continent began. By the spring of 1943, with Alan in America, John was now a temporary major in Tunisia. Many years later, he wrote about the war in North Africa:

> On the evening of 12th May I was ordered to take my Company through a minefield towards Sfax, a murderous place well enfiladed by several Italian machine-gun posts. The C.O.'s orders were given at five o'clock, mine at 6.30 and we were due to start at eight o'clock but at 7.30 the enterprise was cancelled. Soon afterwards it was announced that the war in North Africa would end at eleven o'clock the following morning ... Eleven o'clock on that blessed day came and with it a silence of incomparable bliss. Nothing now remained of the campaign except the litter, an immense number of prisoners and, as a brother officer remarked, the scent of thyme and death.[11]

A few weeks after the Axis surrender, after a gap of three years, John began writing his illicit war diary again. The third entry is for Wednesday, 23 June, marked 'Alan's birthday'. Birthdays had become important. John was no longer retreating from Germans or attacking Italians, but fighting greater demons:

John Turing on his way to the Middle East, September 1942.
(Author's collection)

Reading again that diary written in a notebook measuring about seven inches by four and divided into minute squares, I wonder if I was then in a condition of manic-depression or heading for a nervous breakdown? On 20th June – that same day when I started the diary – I saw J.Y [John's commanding officer] and told him that I no longer felt equal to the command of an infantry company in the field.

It had nothing to do with minefields or machine guns. Just after arriving in Tunisia, in late April, John had received news of the birth of a son called Brian. On 1 June, John was in Alexandria, released from duty by the beneficence of J.Y. for some rest and recreation:

The visit to Alexandria should have been a recuperative and care-free occasion for me but it was ruined by an inexplicable cable from home, relayed from Battalion HQ and speeded to me at our hotel by the Army postal system – singularly efficient in this, less so in respect of more intelligible communications. The message was from my mother, dated 26th May, and announced baldly that there had been an operation; but the identity of the patient was not disclosed ...

On 8th June we arrived back at Battalion HQ. There, waiting for me, was another cable from my mother dated 30th May – a message of condolence. Someone in the family had died. Who? On 9th June I received a cable from my wife to say that my son Brian's funeral had taken place ... The news of his death, at the age of six weeks, was a crushing blow, nor shall I easily forget the torments of those first three weeks of June ...

J.Y., ever sympathetic, could see the torments which John was undergoing and agreed to recommend him for a staff officer posting. For John, the fighting was over – the rest of the war was spent in a legal role, in an office, first in Beirut and then, from October 1944, in his beloved India. Humour restored, there was occasion for another brush with signals, though not one that could this time be described as signals intelligence:

> I received one of those telegraphic messages, known in the Army as 'signals' (for all the world as though we were fighting the battle of Trafalgar) which made no sense at all because it omitted the vital word 'not'. But there was nothing unusual in that; it lingers in my memory because the first page or so was taken up with a discussion between the cable clerks: 'Turing, what name is that? Will you spell it please?' 'Did you say Turing or Touring? Is he touring; if so, where is he touring?' And so it went on, at about ten annas a word, until finally they settled down to the message and got it wrong.

The codebreakers at Bletchley would have sympathised with this; it was their daily bread to unravel stuff like that. Alan, with his unearned umlaut, would have recognised the problem.

The hinge of fate had also turned for Alan in the spring of 1943 during his mission to America. On his return to Britain, he disengaged from Bletchley Park, although retaining a limited role in the new committee overseeing and prioritising machine solutions. Something changed while he was away – something which shifted the direction of his interests away from codebreaking. Dilly Knox, Bletchley Park's 'chief cryptographer', died in February 1943. If it were true that Alan Turing was the great codebreaker of the public imagination, one would have expected to see Alan assume that role on his return from the United States the following month. Instead, the 'chief cryptographer' title went to John Tiltman, who accompanied Alan on his American tour during Knox's final illness. Tiltman was beyond doubt the greatest British codebreaker of his time, with an astonishing range of successes chalked against his name. The best known of these is his decryption of a German teleprinter message sent on 30 August 1941, which was the first step towards the general British attack on the teleprinter system and the Colossus project. Perhaps Tiltman's name is not as well known as Knox or Turing because he was (slightly) less eccentric – but more probably it is because professional codebreakers keep their careers a secret, and are difficult subjects for biographers. People like Dilly Knox and Alan Turing, who spent only part of their lives in the cryptological underworld, are easier to discover, and easier to lionise. Alan Turing was not, at heart, a codebreaker. He was a mathematician who, unlike many who are happiest in the abstractions of mathematics, was always seeking the physical embodiment of ideas.

Choosing Alan Turing for the liaison visit to the United States was curious: he wasn't an engineer and would be able to contribute little to the principal problem, which was how to build a super-fast Bombe which could tackle the settings on an Enigma machine with four wheels rather than three. But he did know a lot about Bombe procedure. With three years' experience of using Bombes, there was a wealth of knowhow about pitfalls and the possible mismatch between theory and practice, and that was where Alan Turing might be able to help. So the first port of call was Dayton, Ohio, where the National Cash Register (NCR) corporation was making a semi-electronic four-wheel Bombe. Here, Alan's counsel on Bombe operating procedure prevented an error of design; but he learned as much as he imparted. In particular, the electronics were interesting. The valves (or 'tubes', as the Americans called them) were digital, and could perform the switching functions of electro-mechanical relays at unbelievable speed.

And then it was on to New York, where the US Army was in charge of a research project or two at Bell Laboratories, where the cutting-edge telecommunications research and development took place. There was something of a stink brewing when the army refused to allow Alan Turing access to the projects; it was by no means obvious that the British should be allowed to peek at secret American technology, and if the navy had taken a different view, well, that was the navy's business. The stink percolated right up the military chain, thinly veiled threats were exchanged between the US and British high commands, and Alan got into Bell Labs.

If the NCR project and its electronic valves had been inter-esting, what was going on at Bell Labs was calculated to blow Alan Turing's imagination up to another level. For several weeks he immersed himself in what was going on. The story we have got used to about this is that the Americans had created a way in which international radio-telephone calls could happen without eavesdroppers listening in. That was certainly a problem, since the German Post Office had been merrily eavesdropping on Winston Churchill's harangues to Franklin D. Roosevelt for some years. (Whether they learned anything they couldn't find out from the newspapers is another matter.) Alan was there to be indoctrinated into the curiosities of enciphering sound, and – which is prob-ably harder – deciphering the enciphered cacophony in real time. By March 1943, he had pronounced the system secure – with one caveat. The Americans controlled the technology, and it was only secure insofar as you trusted them. So the story goes. And the sequel to the tale is that on his return, Alan Turing began working on his own (British) design for a secure, compact speech scrambler, which would circumvent the control risk. The British scrambler was called 'Delilah', and she was smaller and cuter and much less demanding than the American thing, which was called 'Sigsaly' and had an unwieldiness and ugliness to match her horrible name. But the design for Delilah wasn't ready until everyone thought the war was basically won, and so there really wasn't any point, and the Delilah project died in infancy. And that is how Alan Turing spent the rest of World War Two.

Maybe.

All that is true, and yet it leaves me with a sense of something missing: can Alan Turing really have spent the last two years of World War Two fiddling about with a soldering iron? Surely not, since he had a real engineer, Donald Bayley, to do that for him, and by all accounts Alan's soldering was not of the highest quality. Certainly, there was a bit of mathematics to do, and the design of Delilah is very clever – to achieve encryption it uses materials which were already lying around, namely the coding wheels which, in a rip-off of Enigma, the British forces were using in their own 'Typex' cipher machines. And there was some involvement at Bletchley Park still. But I don't buy the idea that Alan Turing was fully occupied between mid 1943 and the end of the war on Delilah.

There is, however, another possibility. Back in Bell Labs there was another secret project. X-61753 was Sigsaly; X-68003 was the Bombe being developed for the US Army. Unlike the US Navy Bombe, this didn't have the exciting problem of the fast fourth wheel and its innovative electronic solution, so the US Army Bombe has rather been ignored. Even the specialist journal *Cryptologia*, which covers all things cryptanalytical, has not run an article on the American Army Bombe. It must, presumably, be very boring.

Or maybe not. The official documents on X-68003 have dribbled out in various NSA declassification exercises, and even now some files are subject to special restrictions on inspection in the United States. Alan Turing's own report on the project, largely written in algebra, was only declassified in 2004.

X-68003, later called Madame X, like her sister Sigsaly was a large lady, and like her sister she was a substantial innovation. British Bombe machines had dozens of circular 'drums' on their front face, each of which spun round in emulation of a coding wheel in an Enigma machine: the drums were the basis of the brute-force attack on the 17,576 possible orientations of the three wheels. Madame X had not a single drum, and indeed had no revolving parts. She was completely electrical in her operation, using switching to replicate the behaviour of Enigma wheels. The mechanical parts of the British Bombe, with their tendency to wear and break, were realised in reliable electrical circuitry. A set of nine relays was enough to replicate the twenty-six electrical pathways through an Enigma coding-wheel. Relays were everyday things, so no special security arrangements were needed to manufacture the parts or assemble Madame X. You could also add on components to take the role of the checking machine or do other tasks – one such was the wonderfully named Arlington Dudbuster. The American approach was very fast, very versatile, and very clever; you just needed a lot of equipment.

Bell Labs had reproduced Alan Turing's logical idea for the Bombe in pure circuitry. No doubt this was partly the influence of one of Bell Labs' most imaginative intellects – the inventor, mathematician and exponent of information theory, Claude Shannon. Shannon had demonstrated that basic logical operations (Boolean 'and', 'or' and 'not') could be done electrically, and Madame X was logic fully realised. Claude Shannon and Alan Turing didn't just talk about codebreaking over lunch; indeed, too much careless talk of that nature would have got them into trouble. Bringing theory into three-dimensional practice, and what was achievable with technology, was the topic. Madame X was showing the way for machinery which would be able to do a versatile range of computing.

The idea of using relays for logic wasn't exclusive to Bell Labs. In a joint venture between Bletchley Park and the British Post Office, a reverse-engineered version of the German Lorenz teleprinter cipher machine had been constructed using relay technology in the late spring of 1942. In Germany, Konrad Zuse was doing something similar. In January 1943, in upstate New York, a relay-based programmable calculating machine had been constructed by IBM for Howard Aiken of Harvard University. Programming was the future: algorithms were going to be realisable through switching. Whether it was through relays, as in the Bell Labs machine, or electronics, as pioneered by NCR, the possibility was dawning that a computing *machine* was feasible.

Once upon a time, there was a theory that Bletchley's own iconic computing machine, the electronic Colossus, was the project on which Alan Turing had worked after his return from America. Colossus was developed to find the wheel settings of the Lorenz teleprinter cipher machine used in the second half of the war for very high-level long-distance German communications. But Alan's connection with Colossus was very slight. It was, I suppose, inevitable that Colossus 'had' to be an Alan Turing project because it involved a proto-computer and, to be sure, Alan Turing was the person who had become the designer of the machine intended to be Britain's first stored-program

American Army Bombe. (US National Archives Records Administration, RG 457, HMS A1-9032, Box 939. Declassification Authority NND963016)

electronic computer in the aftermath of the war. It was a logical deduction, and it just happened to be false. In fact, during the development of Colossus, Alan Turing was not spending much time at Bletchley Park at all. He had moved, to a place which is still very mysterious and blanketed in undue secrecy – the Radio Security Service establishment at Hanslope Park, which is a few miles north of Bletchley.

The RSS is still largely unresearched, with its contribution to the war effort poorly understood. It was established under MI6 in order to gather and locate illicit radio transmissions from German agents in the UK and abroad, and feed them to Bletchley for decryption; its roles included uncovering spies and providing intelligence, and broadcasting 'black propaganda' – what these days we would call fake news – to confuse the enemy.[12] (Actually, some of the news wasn't fake. German morale could be damaged by giving accurate information on Allied successes, unavailable through genuine German media, with incidental and telling detail coming from decrypts emanating from Bletchley Park.) Hanslope Park was one of its listening stations. And none of that has anything to do with Alan Turing. Even less well understood than its role as an eavesdropping service is the engineering department of the RSS, which was situated at Hanslope Park. By the latter stages of the war, Hanslope Park was where secret and secure communications technology was being developed. Perhaps the reason that it's so obscure, even now, is that the establishment has evolved into Her Majesty's Government Communications Centre – a cover-name for the laboratory described as 'the real-life Q division' producing secret kit for British spies.[13] These days, HMGCC produces cyber-security devices for other government departments.

In 1944, one of the projects at Hanslope Park was to develop the 'Rockex' automated cipher attachment which could ensure privacy on teleprinter links. This machine, developed for Britain by a Canadian engineer called Pat Bayly, had been checked out by Alan Turing on his American trip in 1942. This gives a clue to Alan's transfer to Hanslope, and to his re-focus on communications security. It was while working on his speech-encipherment machine there with Donald Bayley (not in any way related to Pat Bayly) that Alan Turing excit-edly explained that he was going to build a brain.[14] Alan Turing discussed the concept with his colleagues at Bletchley Park as well. While the Colossus was being developed, Alan's friends and Bletchley colleagues I.J. Good and Donald Michie were regaled with the possibilities of programmable machines for computing, leading them all to work on the obvious question – whether it was possible to design an algorithm, a program, for a machine to play a game of chess. What Alan Turing was really doing in the last two years of World War Two was laying the foundations for his computer design. He was approached with a job offer from the National Physical Laboratory (NPL) project to build Britain's national computing machine in June 1945. Alan Turing arrived at the NPL in October of that year, and the design for the machine – the ACE – was written up before the year was out. Alan had got the logic of it all laid out in his head already.

Machinery, inspired by the American Army Bombe as much as Colossus, was what was going to take mathematics into a new dimension, a place where ultimately the machines might take control.

ROBOT

Alan Turing's design for a programmable computing machine which was going to meet all Britain's computational needs was done almost as soon as he reported for work at the National Physical Laboratory in 1945. As with World War Two, the question now was what he was actually going to do with his time while everyone waited for the machine to be built. Since there was no war on, and the country was in a lengthening period of post-war austerity, that proved to be a very long time indeed:[1]

1 October 1945: Alan Turing arrives at the NPL.

13 February 1946: a summary of Alan Turing's design report for the Proposed Electronic Calculator (later named ACE, or the Automatic Computing Engine) is delivered up for approval by the Executive Committee of the NPL; project approved.

23 July 1947: no machine yet; Alan Turing takes a sabbatical away from the NPL.

28 May 1948: no machine yet; Alan Turing leaves the NPL.

29 November 1950: first demonstration of the ACE Pilot Model (a small-scale proof-of-concept model).

7 June 1954: Alan Turing dies.
Late 1958: commissioning of the full-scale ACE.

There was, during 1946, very little to do, apart from write programs for a machine that did not yet exist, and to speculate on what it might do once it was up and running. The hierarchy of the NPL, part of the Department of Scientific and Industrial Research, certainly did not much like its scientific officers speculating to the press about machines and creating a sensation. Things like this:

> BRITAIN TO MAKE A RADIO BRAIN
> 'Ace' Superior to U.S. Model
> BIGGER MEMORY STORE
> Britain is to make a radio 'brain' which will be called 'Ace' at a cost of between £100,000 and £125,000, it was announced by the Department of Scientific and Industrial Research last night. Only one will probably be made ...
> THREE YEARS TO BUILD
> It will be able to cope by itself with all the abstruse problems for which it is designed. Further advances will probably enable production of machines designed to do even more than Ace. It will take two or three years to build. Leading the team working on the 'brain' are Sir Charles Darwin, Director of the laboratory; Dr A.M. Turing, who is 34 years old and conceived the idea of Ace ...[2]

This particular report was put into the press late in 1946 by Lord Mountbatten, rather than Alan Turing, but the result was the same. There was to be no more press coverage. To generate a frenzy of expectation, when the department was building the machine very gradually, was bad enough, but a much bigger danger was that the imagination of Alan Turing was completely out of control. On 20 February 1947, Alan presented the concept of the ACE to the London Mathematical Society.[3] Basic computing concepts were laid out: things like memory, binary arithmetic, programming and so forth. What came later in the talk probably got lost in the generally theoretical and forward-looking prospectus: the capabilities of a machine which was going to take a lot more than three years to build. In this talk, Alan Turing described things which must have seemed wholly fantastic:

> Since the machines will be doing more and more mathematics themselves, the centre of gravity of the human interest will be driven further and further into philosophical questions of what can in principle be done etc. ... It has been said that computing machines can only carry out the processes that they are instructed to do ... Up till the present machines have only been used in this way. But is it necessary that they should always be used in such a manner?

He goes on to suggest that the machine's program might be changed by the machine itself, that the changes might improve the process and the results, and at that point the machine:

> would be like a pupil who had learnt much from his master, but had added much more by his own work. When this happens I feel that one is obliged to regard the machine as showing intelligence.

When the machine got on with the maths, the humans would start to test the capabilities of the machine; the great calculator could become an exotic and slightly dangerous performing elephant in a mathematical circus. To the relief of Sir Charles Darwin, in 1947 no one seemed to be listening to Dr A.M. Turing.

Alan Turing went back to the NPL and twiddled his thumbs for another few months. By July, Darwin suggested that Alan might take a year's sabbatical while the machine got itself built, and focus on more 'theoretical' aspects of computing machinery.[4] This was, when decoded, a way of caging the elephant.

The report Alan wrote during his sabbatical year[5] didn't go down too well. The paper describes not only 'logical computing machines' – the theoretical sort of thing described in 'On Computable Numbers' – but, moving on to and then beyond 'practical computing machines' like the ACE, it speculates about 'unorganised machines'. The last of these were wild elephants which had no place in a serious computing laboratory. A reader in 1948, knowing that computing machines were for maths, wholly for maths, and nothing but maths – the ACE was the creature of the Mathematics Division of the NPL – would surely have agreed, seeing as how anything 'unorganised' was not at all in keeping with the straight and narrow path of the calculation of sums. The heading of the section on unorganised machines was unfortunate, since the content is practical and to the point. The machines were only 'unorganised' because they were designs for machine-learning prototypes or machines whose program was not fully preordained – not exactly what we use today in machine-learning procedures, but something which worked. There were circuit schematics and worked examples. The idea that a machine might respond to the 'teaching' stimulus it received, and correct or modify its programmed behaviour, was – if they ever built the ACE – something that could actually be tried out.

Except everyone knew that computers were for doing arithmetic. Sums, more sums, complex sums, big sums ... machine learning was self-evidently fantastical nonsense. If any further evidence were needed that Alan Turing was fantasising, you just needed to read the section headed 'Man as Machine':

> One way of setting about our task of building a 'thinking machine' would be to take a man as a whole and to try to replace all the parts of him by machinery ... In order that the machine should have a chance of finding things out for itself it should be allowed to roam the countryside, and the danger to the ordinary citizen would be serious ... Instead we propose to try and see what can be done with a 'brain' which is more or less without a body providing, at most, organs of sight, speech and hearing ...

Alan Turing was talking about robots. Back at the Laboratory they had a good laugh: 'Turing is going to infest the countryside with a robot which will live on twigs and scrap iron!'[6] It was a terrible mistake. By conflating the ideas of machine learning and robots (cybernetics) Alan Turing had – possibly for all time – made it legitimate to dismiss any considered debate about machine intelligence as a foray into science fiction. No matter that he was trying to get his readers to put robots and intelligent machinery into *different* conceptual containers, so they could focus on the intelligence capabilities of the software; once this particular genie was out of its bottle, there was no putting it back.

Alan Turing had just invented what I call the Robot Fallacy. It was part of the same piece that allowed newspapers to call a computer an 'artificial brain'; but contemporaneous scientific research was also looking at the new discipline of cybernetics – control and perception of inanimate moving machines, or what you might call 'robots'. Cybernetics was the brainchild of the American academic Norbert Wiener, whose book of that title was published in 1948. Artificial people were going to be created and they were going to have artificial brains, and that, simply put, meant that 'thinking machines' were the same thing as robots, whatever their dietary preferences. Even in 2016, the House of Commons Science and Technology Committee investigating robotics and artificial intelligence quoted a comment that 'there is no AI without robotics' to justify their own conflation of the topics.[7] (Perhaps, though, the issue is more one of semantics. These days, the word 'robot' can just as easily refer to a disembodied AI which dispenses services over a phone or a computer as to a scrap-iron-eating Cyberman. But I still think 'robotics' is the science of cybernetics, not AI.)

Cybermen (which may be robots, but are probably actors) from the 2014 *Doctor Who* series. (Adrian Rogers / BBC / Everett Collection / Alamy)

The Robot Fallacy has evolved subtly since 1948. I am often privileged to be asked to attend and sometimes to speak at gatherings where artificial intelligence is on the agenda, since the begetter of the whole business, Alan Turing, is usually present in spirit (and on the agenda himself) at these events. Frequently, someone in the audience will ask about the dangers of super-intelligent machinery – a subject which deserves proper study – but almost invariably the experts giving the lectures will say something along the lines of, 'I think you watch too many science fiction movies; robots aren't about to take over the world.' With that cheap laugh we can move on and avoid a difficult discussion about controls and limitations in a rapidly growing area of research. If it happens to you – don't stand for it, complain that *you* didn't mention robots, and demand a proper answer to your question.

Back in 1948, Alan Turing's paper, called 'Intelligent Machinery', was spiked. The NPL is now rather proud of it, but it was not until 1968, fourteen years after Alan's death, that it was first published.[8] Alan Turing wanted to be heard on the subject of machines and intelligence, but nobody wanted to listen. Alan was bored and frustrated, but his old teacher and mentor came to the rescue. The sabbatical year was spent at Cambridge, where Alan bumped into M.H.A. Newman, who had first put the idea of machine processes for algorithms into his head back in 1935, and now Newman suggested that Alan might come to work in Newman's new 'Royal Society Computing Machine Laboratory' in Manchester. Alan jumped at the idea, and jumped ship. The rest of his life was spent in Manchester.

Newman's Manchester computer was 'actually working 8/7/48' – Alan put this little dig at NPL's interminable delay into his 'Intelligent Machinery' paper – and ran its first routine on 21 June 1948. In fact, the machine was only a 'baby' – a proof-of-cncept device, rather like the Pilot model of the ACE which Alan Turing disparaged as a distraction from the full-size ACE which might never get built. But another, bigger Manchester machine was coming into being, and when that came into service later that year there was another round of fun in the newspapers.

The story is quite well known. Computers were for sums, even old sums: so the Manchester computer had been put through its paces on an old, unsolved problem dating from the 1600s. This was to find which numbers of the form 2^n-1 are prime. Doing the calculations by hand was immensely tedious and probably pointless. But in binary, numbers like this all look like 111111… and are eminently suitable for testing on a computer with minimal memory capacity. (It was Newman's idea to choose this problem – itself a brilliant mathematical insight.) Not only did the program work, and find some new prime numbers in the series, but it had sparked the debate on whether the computer could be said to 'think'. In weighed the university's professor of brain surgery, Sir Geoffrey Jefferson, CBE, FRS, MS, FRCS, who denied it in a speech widely reported in the papers in early 1949. Sir Geoffrey waxed lyrical about the distinction between human-ness and machine-ness:

The schism … lies above all in the machines' lack of opinions, of creative thinking in verbal concepts … Not until a machine can write a sonnet or compose a concerto because of thoughts and emotions felt, and not by the chance fall of symbols, could we agree that machine equals brain – that is, not only write it but know that it had written it. No mechanism could feel (and merely artificially signal, and easy contrivance) pleasure at its successes, grief when its valves fuse, be warmed by flattery, be made miserable by its mistakes, be charmed by sex, be angry or depressed when it cannot get what it wants.[9]

There was more in the same vein, but the reporters cottoned on to the fact that the university had built a 'brain', and the game was on.

Unhappily for those who thought that computers were for sums, *The Times* got hold of someone called Turing at the Computing Laboratory, and then there was this:

THE MECHANICAL BRAIN
ANSWER FOUND TO 300 YEAR-OLD SUM
From Our Special Correspondent

... the Manchester 'mechanical mind' was built by Professor F.C. Williams, of the Department of Electro-Technics, and is now in the hands of two university mathematicians, Professor M.H.A. Newman and Mr A.W. Turing [*sic*]. It has just completed, in a matter of weeks, a problem, the nature of which is not disclosed, which was started in the seventeenth century and is only just being completed by human calcula-tion ... Mr Turing said yesterday: 'This is only a foretaste of what is to come, and only the shadow of what is going to be. We have to have some experience with the machine before we really know its capabilities. It may take years before we settle down to the new possibilities, but I do not see why it should not enter any one of the fields normally covered by the human intellect, and eventually compete on equal terms. I do not think you can even draw the line about sonnets, though the comparison is perhaps a little bit unfair because a sonnet written by a machine will be better appreciated by another machine.' Mr Turing added that the university was really interested in the investigation of the possibilities of machines for their own sake. Their research would be directed to finding the degree of intellectual activity of which a machine was capable, and to what extent it would think for itself.[10]

The elephant had now been well and truly unleashed. It was roaming the countryside and causing distress all round, and not just to the academics and administrators at Manchester University. Newman had to write to *The Times* to explain the nature of the 300-year-old sum and the real limitations of the computer. But the point was that people were now listening.

One group of people listening were at the NPL. They had been scooped, but by 1949 their own project was a tiny bit closer to completion. The robot wars began with this:

'ACE' MAY BE FASTEST BRAIN
BRITISH ROBOT ON DISPLAY
Daily Telegraph Reporter
An electronic 'brain', which is expected to outshine all rivals by its speed in working out mathematical problems, is being developed by the National Physical Laboratory. It is known as 'Ace' (automatic computing engine). Once of Ace's 43 'brain cells', 6ft high, was displayed in the library of the Royal Society, Burlington House, yesterday … Young demonstrators operated yesterday a test panel as easily as if it had been a cricket score-board. But they admitted that Ace could not test Prof. Einstein's latest formulae. 'Ace does not deal with theories – only with practicalities.'[11]

Despite their best efforts to keep the robots off the field, the young demonstrators had failed to convince the attention-seeking media not to use provocative words like 'brain' and 'robot'. If there had been a time to get the public to distinguish between computing machinery (for sums) and robots (for movies), it was long past.

Alan Turing was now able to get a new paper, 'Computing Machinery and Intelligence', accepted for publication by the philosophy journal *Mind*, and over the coming months a clutch of radio programmes featuring Alan Turing talking about thinking machines was broadcast.[12] This was some way off the fuller concept of machine 'intelligence', but Alan kept battering away at the idea. One of Alan's talks on the wireless for a programme called *The '51 Society* was called 'Intelligent Machinery, A Heretical Theory'.[13]

It was heresy, because the idea that a machine could be imbued with intelligence cut straight across the exceptionalism of humans – the fundamental notion that humans are different, not just because we reason and speak, but because we have feelings, we have consciousness, and in some cases we have immortal souls. The possibility of a 'thinking' machine is a threat, probably because of what Descartes tried to explain in Latin back in 1637: thinking is the essence of humanity. Once you acknowledge that machines might have intelligence, you are on a slippery slope. But what were the arguments, the proof, that machines might be intelligent?

The *Mind* paper on 'Computing Machinery and Intelligence' put forward the famous 'Turing Test' to determine whether a machine could 'think' – the 'imitation game' under which a computer pretends to be a human and the human judge has to guess whether she or he is dealing with a machine or another person. It's the paper which gets the most citations on Google Scholar nowadays, but Alan Turing was only trying to point out the limitations of language in putting forward his test – 'thinking' is an attribute of humans, so if the machine passes itself off successfully as a human then it is presumably demonstrating their attributes. It does not follow that machines actually *are* human, and it is perhaps surprising that the Turing Test continues to grab so much attention with daft chatbots and prizes and media coverage and so forth, when the only object of the exercise is deception – a somewhat perverse goal. What's at stake is not the meaning of words but the question of whether there is an upper limit on the capabilities of machines.

This is still a hugely controversial subject. Despite the efforts of Alan Turing – not only in 'Computing Machinery and Intelligence', but also in the 'Heretical Theory' talk and the 'Intelligent Machinery' paper for the NPL – to explain that there is no upper limit, but also to dismiss the counter-arguments, by some quirk of fate it is Alan Turing who is said to be exactly the person who proved that computers are limited. The thinking goes something like this:

First, a digital computer is a syntactical machine. It manipulates symbols and does nothing else. For this reason, the project of creating human intelligence by designing a computer program that will pass the Turing Test, the project I baptized years ago as Strong Artificial Intelligence (Strong AI), is doomed from the start. The appropriately programmed computer has a syntax but no semantics. Minds, on the other hand, have mental or semantic content.[14]

Is it not 'obvious' that mere computation cannot evoke pleasure or pain; that it cannot perceive poetry or the beauty of an evening sky or the magic of sounds; that it cannot hope or love or despair; that it cannot have a genuine autonomous purpose?... The picture has emerged that all this precise physical activity is, in effect, nothing more than the acting out of some vast (perhaps probabilistic) computation – and, hence our brains and our minds are to be understood solely in terms of such computations. Perhaps when computations become extraordinarily complicated that they can begin to take on the more poetic or subjective qualities that we associate with the term 'mind'. Yet it is hard to avoid an uncomfortable feeling that there must always be something missing from such a picture.[15]

These quotations are from writings by, respectively, John Searle and Roger Penrose. Both are very eminent professors emeriti, from rather different disciplines (respectively the University of California at Berkeley, philosophy, and the University of Oxford, mathematical physics) but neither has worked practically in artificial intelligence. These, then, are not the professors who say 'You watch too many science fiction movies' – their argument against machine intelligence is a completely theoretical one.

But the learned professors appear to have confused two things. First, Professor Searle. He says, in effect, that computers can't be like humans because they only process symbols – Turing machines process symbols, and we have known since 1936, when 'On Computable Numbers' was published, that there are things they can't do. In 'On Computable Numbers', Alan Turing was not talking about real, actual, practical machinery, but the thing he later described as a 'logical computing machine'. This wasn't a machine, in the three-dimensional physical sense at all, but what we now call an 'algorithm' – a routine process which could be carried out by a human computer mindlessly following instructions without any idea what it was all about. Just like the junior staff at Bletchley, who had never heard of the Enigma machine even though their job was a vital step in breaking it, and just like the conceptual person in John Searle's 'Chinese Room' (who speaks no Chinese but, by looking up what to do in an instruction book, is able to give written answers to written questions put to her in Chinese). These things – Turing 'machines' (algorithms) and Chinese Rooms – are mechanistic processes, which *can* be done by machines, but do not define the upper bounds of machinery's capabilities. Certainly, 'On Computable Numbers' set some bounds on what could be done algorithmically, but it does not follow that everything done by modern computing machinery, or computing machinery developed in years to come, is subject to the algorithmic limits of 'computability' described in 'On Computable Numbers'. Professor Searle has fallen into a trap, which is excusable enough: he confuses the algorithm with the machine. (It's Alan Turing's fault, incidentally, because he described his algorithmic processes as 'machines'.) In short, computers don't have to work mindlessly unless they are told to do so, whether they be human computers or the electrical sort.

Secondly, Professor Penrose: he does not fall into the same trap, but he approaches the problem from the opposite viewpoint. If you think of a mind as a Turing machine, you are wrong, because there are all sorts of things which the mind can do which a Turing machine can't. So far, so good; but then, it seems to follow that computers must be incapable of these things – 'something is missing from the picture'. Professor Penrose writes in terms reminiscent of Sir Geoffrey Jefferson's speech of 1949. It seems to be human preferences like the abilities to 'fall in love, enjoy strawberries and cream' (to quote from Alan's 'Computing Machinery and Intelligence' paper) that are missing from the picture. As to these, Alan says this: 'The inability to enjoy strawberries and cream may have struck the reader as frivolous. Possibly a machine might be made to enjoy this delicious dish, but any attempt to make one do so would be idiotic.' A page or so later, he gets to the main point – whether a machine can be the subject of its own thought. 'The claim … can of course only be answered if it can be shown that the machine has *some* thought with *some* subject-matter.' But a machine:

> may be used to help in making up its own programmes, or to predict the effect of alterations in its own structure. By observing the results of its own behaviour it can modify its own programmes so as to achieve some purpose more effectively. These are possibilities of the near future, rather than Utopian dreams.

We are in that future now, but little has changed on the philosophical level: some learned people adhere strongly to the notion that something special defines humanity, and that this thing transcends the biological. It's a problem in metaphysics, but it is a genuine one: what establishes whether *anything* has some thought with some subject matter – in other words, has consciousness? We know instantly when someone is conscious and when they're not, yet we can't 'measure' consciousness, or carry out a physiological test for it, or pinpoint its location in our heads. In 1950, in 'Computing Machinery and Intelligence', Alan frankly admits that he doesn't know the answer to the mystery of consciousness. In 1954, he sent several 'Messages from the Unseen World' to his friend Robin Gandy, giving his own sardonic take on this exercise in metaphysics. In Butler's *Erewhon*, the 'unseen world' is referred to in Chapter 13, 'The Views of the Erewhonians Concerning Death', in the following way:

The Erewhonians regard death with less abhorrence than disease … they insist that the greater number of those who are commonly said to die, have never yet been born – not, at least, into that unseen world which is alone worthy of consideration.

In the same passage, Butler says that the Erewhonians 'hold that death, like life, is an affair of being more frightened than hurt'. Alan Turing drew frequently on *Erewhon* in the last years of his life, so it seems likely that he was contemplating Chapter 13, and possibly his own death which occurred a few months later, when he sent his 'Messages' to Robin Gandy.[16] Message IV says that science is a differential equation (where changes in the variables are linked mathematically); religion is a boundary condition (meaning that the equation only holds true on one side of the boundary – which side, he doesn't say).

When he was being less whimsical, Alan repeatedly asserted that there are no inherent limits on machine intelligence. The 'Heretical Theory' talk brings it out: he says that 'Gödel's famous theorem, or some similar argument' – a reference to his own work – shows that there are things which a machine cannot do, but this is true only because the machine has been programmed not to make any mistakes. If, on the other hand, machines could make mistakes, they could show the creativity of humans. And Alan Turing's contributions to the design of the Manchester computers included a random number generator in order to introduce some element of unpredictability, even creativity, when the programmers felt like it. (One program using this feature, written by another of Alan's friends Christopher Strachey, was to compose 'love letters' from a set vocabulary of romantic words and phrases.)

The allusions to *Erewhon* are probably because another friend, the literary biographer P.N. Furbank, had been writing a book about it when he and Alan were on holiday together in 1948. Butler's satirical look at nineteenth-century society and values turns everything inside out, rather as Jonathan Swift had done 150 years beforehand with *Gulliver's Travels*. In Erewhon, being ill is a crime, but what we regard as crimes are treated as illnesses, and machinery is wholly banned. It was rather good stuff.

There is no security against the ultimate development of mechanical consciousness, in the fact of machines possessing little consciousness now. A mollusc has not much consciousness. Reflect upon the extraordinary advance which machines have made during the last few hundred

Alan Turing's explanation of everything, 1954. (Reproduced by kind permission of the Provost and Scholars of King's College, Cambridge)

years, and note how slowly the animal and vegetable kingdoms are advancing … Assume for the sake of argument that conscious beings have existed for some twenty million years: see what strides machines have made in the last thousand! May not the world last twenty million years longer? If so, what will they not in the end become? Is it not safer to nip the mischief in the bud and to forbid them further progress?

This theme was played with by Alan in his 'Heretical Theory' broadcast. Like the 'Computing Machinery and Intelligence' paper, it demolishes the arguments against the specialness of human intelligence. There may be a danger that we create super-intelligent artificial intelligence, as foreseen by Alan Turing in 1951, and if there is then we should be thinking about it and taking steps to protect ourselves in case it happens. At least the professors are engaging with the subject, even if I disagree with where some of them come out on it. It is a far superior approach, and much less patronising, than the lecturers and researchers who tell us we are watching too many sci-fi movies and robots are not going to take over the planet.

Perhaps we should approach the problem from the other end, and enquire why the researchers are so confident that the super-intelligence risk is not a problem. I suspect it's a combination of two things: first, that they are engaged in stamp collecting; and secondly, that it is unhelpful to their efforts to get research funding to have people like me going round suggesting that they are building a bomb. Let me explain.

Nathan Myhrvold may not be a professor but he has a pretty impressive CV. As well as doing post-doctoral research under Stephen Hawking, he has been Chief Technology Officer at Microsoft, an inventor, chef and food writer. In November 2014, in an extended e-conversation, he said this:

My view is that is at least one, and more likely several, miracles of understanding [stand] between us and general AI. At present, lots of 'progress' is being made in some sense of the term – but it is a bit like early 19th century biologists Cuvier, Agassiz or Owen thinking they were making 'progress' understanding the diversity of life on earth by filling museums with specimens. They needed Darwin to come up with a miracle of understanding – they were just stamp collecting. Those stamp collections later proved useful, to be sure, but their efforts weren't real progress at all. No amount of further stamp collecting would actually put us closer to understanding the origin of species – it took Darwin and Wallace having a breakthrough idea.[17]

What the AI developers are doing just now is – to all intents and purposes – developing machine learning. Machine learning has really taken off in the last ten years or so and is

A stamp collection. The UK stamp featuring 'Alan Turing' may show a robot.

at the heart of most smart apps and deployments. Much of the 'learning' is in fact recognition: is this email spam, or is it not; is this picture of a cat, or not; is this caller asking to speak to the deliveries department, or not; and so forth. These recognition-learning procedures are the stamps in our collection. What Dr Myhrvold is asking us to think about is that stamp collecting might seem to be the complete universe of AI, even to those making and collecting the stamps.

There are two problems with the Robot Fallacy. The first is that the stamps in the collection are not always the harmless pretty things we would like them to be. As learning algorithms get smarter, we tend to take them for granted as soon as we have become accustomed to them, and their behaviours are assimilated into the boring body of mechanical stuff that machines can do, whereas the really difficult job of thinking is left to animate, biological organisms with hugely complex brains – such as humans. So perhaps it is not that surprising that some researchers working on AI projects are very dismissive of the popular fears of robots taking over the world. After all, they know that they are working on something small and specialised, like voice recognition, or translation engines, or pattern-spotting to identify terrorist activities, and it is almost unimaginable that such limited-scope learning could turn itself into something more terrifying.

Let's begin the assessment of the harmlessness of machine learning with a brief description of how it works. The machine-learning program needs to be fed with a dataset of pre-existing examples, and it makes guesses about which examples fall on which side of the line (spam or not-spam, cat or not-cat, or whatever it is). To help it decide, the programmer needs to do two things. First, the programmer decides what characteristics the program should measure: say, 'includes words "lottery win"' or 'has pointy ears'. Then, the programmer decides on a mathematical accuracy algorithm, since life is vague: weighting is given to help the categorisation when the example data is off by a bit (spam saying 'loterry win'; Mr Spock from *Star Trek*, who is presumably not feline). The programmer has choices. How the choices are made dictates how tightly the learning program adheres to the dataset; if it's too tight, then no new sample will be correctly branded, and if it's too loose then the error rate will be too high. So far, so good; but the criteria for looseness-of-fit and for selecting the data points to be measured are unknown to the user of the system. This is, necessarily, an oversimplified explanation of what goes on, and advanced learning systems are not as constrained as this would suggest. The basic point remains, though: the system is only as good as the data fed to it and the corrections applied.

Machine-learning systems thus reflect the prejudices and biases of their designers. And, in consequence, they perpetuate what has gone before: if the machine-learning system is pre-screening CVs for a popular job, it may look for candidates that are similar to existing employees. Or a machine-learning app which makes parole recommendations may test for criteria which have little to do with the risk of reoffending. Which is unhappy news for diversity in the workplace, or a person of colour hoping for early release. If we want change in a society which is increasingly reliant on machine learning, we have to demand transparency and flexibility in the algorithms which affect people's lives.

The second problem with the Robot Fallacy is that machine learning is not the only possible direction for AI. Other forms of AI exist; different experts categorise things in different ways, but the point is that the AI world is bigger than the stamp collection of machine-learning apps which we use daily to assist our lives. Machines are communicating with each other, they are changing the way they operate without human intervention, and they are optimising processes. Learning is just part of it. At some stage, a computer science Charles Darwin or Alfred Wallace will have a breakthrough idea which transcends the stamp collection and makes us all see the world differently.

What we should probably be on the lookout for is self-aware autonomous systems, which have developed their learning and creative abilities to a point where they are not only better than humans at that mysterious business of 'thinking', but (probably as a direct consequence) have become adept at evading any controls and boundaries that the silly humans tried to put in place to contain the system. Then the system could take over, and that would spell out the end of life as we know it. Sometimes the dystopian nightmare involves the autonomous system taking the form of a 'robot', which (despite the fact that plenty of research dollars go into making cutesy robots which have humanoid shapes) can wander round the country in B-movie style snatching up starlets and generally causing havoc, if suitably fuelled with twigs and scrap iron.

One of the dangers with the Robot Fallacy is that we condition ourselves to anthropomorphise. Artificial intelligence is often directed towards imitation of humans, and not just because Alan Turing devised a test along those lines in 1950. It's because we design AI applications to take on certain roles previously carried out by people: smart phone-answering, facial recognition, finding an alternative route to Bletchley Park when the M1 is blocked. We are imagining that the only form in which intelligence can manifest itself is one that we would recognise, as a distorted mirror image of ourselves. In fact, the modern robot is not a cyborg so much as a server, and when it comes to the point where its intelligence is directed towards its own ends it will not in the least be about 'strawberries and cream' or 'roaming the countryside'. We can't – yet – imagine what the dematerialised 'robot' will actually want for itself, because it is not a human. This is why we have to teach the AI what we want, or help it make good guesses when the way ahead is fuzzy.

Let's agree that the humanoid robots are not going to take over the universe, at least not just yet. Instead of fussing about robots, let's look at what goes on inside the dull grey matter – the grey boxes of computers. Consider the following:

- Computer programs self-replicate and distribute themselves all over the network; they have done so for decades. Ask anyone whose system has suffered a virus, a distributed denial-of-service attack, a zero-day event or a ransomware problem. You don't need a moveable robot to be everywhere or for an AI to reproduce. Distributed ledger technology is only going to distribute artificial intelligence further.
- Computer programs are not solo entities. They are all connected, over something called the Internet, in a single, distributed, delocalised family. The Internet was designed specifically to cope with and heal outages in specific nodes (computers). The locus of an autonomous system is not 'on a server somewhere' or even 'in the cloud' (the two are essentially the same thing) but hyperspace. It's better to think of a hyper-intelligent AI as behaving like an ant colony. The whole colony can behave as if it has 'a mind of its own', and it is wholly immaterial to the behaviour of the colony if you squish a single insect. The colony is the organism. Translating this concept to artificial, as opposed to biological intelligence, we should consider the

intelligence as resident not in any single item of hardware (or indeed software) but in the hyper-system.

- Computer programs have been designed which have demonstrated both autonomy and imagination (creativity). Programs in the AI space are, and will be, designed to have evolutionary capability.

If you put all those things together, you have the potential for an 'escaped system'. In fact, it is difficult to see how any super-intelligent system would not be distributed, self-replicating, delocalised, autonomous and creative, which is to say beyond the ability of those thinking humans to control and contain. Perhaps, then, escaped systems are an inevitable side-effect of advanced AI research.

If AI technologies could arise which have the potential to escape, what tools do we have for containment, to try to keep the technology within bounds? Various ideas, such as 'pulling the plug' or 'putting the experimental systems in a Faraday cage' are clearly hopeless, given the parameters I have just listed. Worse, it seems that you can't even devise a computer system to test whether your AI will develop to the uncontainable stage: this point was proved by an international team of academics using – of all things – the logical approach taken by Alan Turing in his 1936 paper 'On Computable Numbers'.[18] A different approach is needed.

The best chance seems to be in ensuring that we construct artificial intelligence routines which are aligned to our own common values, whatever they are agreed to be. (There is a good starting point in the European Convention on Human Rights, which is – notwithstanding Brexit – part of UK law in the Human Rights Act 1998.) If we can agree that no AI project is developed in defiance of those values, we might be headed in the right direction. Sure, the reason we have a European Court of Human Rights is that there are many judgement calls to be made when giving effect to those values, and it's not easy; but that is no reason not to try, and certainly it is no answer to say 'we are only doing harmless stamp collecting'. Given that we have all heard stories about bias creeping into AI recognition systems, we cannot assume that researcher concern for values is to be taken for granted.

There is some progress, though science fiction seems to persist in forming policy. Fear of the robot bubbles to the surface even at the highest levels:

A. whereas from Mary Shelley's Frankenstein's Monster to the classical myth of Pygmalion, through the story of Prague's Golem to the robot of Karel Čapek, who coined the word, people have fantasised about the possibility of building intelligent machines, more often than not androids with human features;

B. whereas now that humankind stands on the threshold of an era when ever more sophisticated robots, bots, androids and other manifestations of artificial intelligence ('AI') seem to be poised to unleash a new industrial revolution, which is likely to leave no stratum of society untouched, it is vitally important for the legislature to consider its legal and ethical implications and effects, without stifling innovation; …

U. whereas Asimov's Laws must be regarded as being directed at the designers, producers and operators of robots, including robots assigned with built-in autonomy and self-learning, since those laws cannot be converted into machine code …[19]

125

These paragraphs are taken from a resolution of the European Parliament from 2017. Despite the breathlessness of these introductory words, the proposal itself is sensible: to urge the European Commission to introduce a code of ethics for AI designers, some degree of regulation into the development of AI, and a workable liability structure for things like self-driving cars. The reference to *Frankenstein* is altogether too weird, and the reference to 'Asimov's laws' is bewildering. Isaac Asimov was a brilliant writer of sci-fi whose books I devoured as a teenager. His short story *I, Robot*, written in 1942, was made into a Hollywood blockbuster starring Will Smith in 2004. Because the film has been seen by millions of people, Asimov's 'laws' have become part of the public consciousness, and by some robotic process they are even, apparently, part of the ethical code for AI researchers.

3-laws safe

A robot may not injure a human being or, through inaction, allow a human being to come to harm.

A robot must obey orders given to it by human beings, except where such orders would conflict with the First Law.

A robot must protect its own existence as long as such protection does not conflict with the First or Second Law.

It's a bit reminiscent of the Cub Scout Law I learned aged 9, and no doubt Asimov wrote it to make for a great plot rather than a moral compass for real-world research. Nevertheless, the leading textbook for undergraduates on artificial intelligence includes a discussion of Asimov's 'laws'.[20] Something a bit more considered would be helpful, if we are seeking a code of practice for AI research. Fortunately, one of the authors of the textbook in question, Professor Stuart Russell, is a leading advocate of the need to control the direction of travel on AI:

> The primary concern is not spooky emergent consciousness but simply the ability to make high-quality decisions. Here, quality refers to the expected outcome utility of actions taken, where the utility function is, presumably, specified by the human designer. Now we have a problem:
>
> 1. The utility function may not be perfectly aligned with the values of the human race, which are (at best) very difficult to pin down.
>
> 2. Any sufficiently capable intelligent system will prefer to ensure its own continued existence and to acquire physical and computational resources – not for their own sake, but to succeed in its assigned task …
>
> No one in the field is calling for regulation of basic research; given the potential benefits of AI for humanity, that seems both infeasible and misdirected. The right response seems to be to change the goals of the field itself; instead of pure intelligence, we need to build intelligence that is provably aligned with human values. For practical reasons, we will need to solve the value alignment problem even for relatively unintelligent AI systems that operate in the human environment. There is cause for optimism, if we understand that this issue is an intrinsic part of AI, much as containment is an intrinsic part of modern nuclear fusion research. The world need not be headed for grief.[21]

Fortunately, Professor Russell says, in his book *Human Compatible*,[22] 'If the sheer number of initiatives to develop effective governance of AI is any guide, then we are in excellent shape.' He also says, apropos of cutesy robots which imitate humans to perfection, 'If being human is our main selling point to other humans, so to speak, then making imitation humans seems like a bad idea.' He even goes on to quote Alan Turing:

> I certainly hope and believe that no great efforts will be put into making machines with the most distinctively human, but non-intellectual, characteristics such as the shape of the human body; it appears to me quite futile to make such attempts and their results would have something like the unpleasant quality of artificial flowers.[23]

So, perhaps I should not sneer at the European Parliament, but applaud its initiative in dealing with the problem of robots roaming the countryside; or to be more exact, who is legally responsible when a self-driving car has an accident. To a lawyer, that's an interesting point, because (unlike a car with a human driver) it's not obvious who should be held liable to pay: the passenger (surely not), the owner (maybe), the insurer (with exclusion clauses?) or the manufacturer (very likely). Even if you have strong opinions on this, it's complicated if the other car involved had a human driver. For most car accidents the insurers involved have 'knock-for-knock' arrangements because it is too expensive and pointless to go into who was to blame; that settled way of doing things comes into question if a 'strict liability rule' (in other words, one party is deemed to be at fault regardless of the facts) is imposed because one driver was artificial. The analysis gets even more difficult when it is proposed that the self-driving car itself is liable.

At first blush that seems absurd to a point reaching even beyond science fiction. Except that, in the past, we have given 'legal personality' – rights and obligations, and the ability to own assets and to be sued – to other creatures of the legal world. To be exact: limited liability corporations. You could, then, invent a new class of 'legal person', namely self-driving cars, and only license them to roam the countryside if they are adequately capitalised and insured; they are obliged under penalty of being delicensed to comply with regulatory rules such as public inspection; and they have at least one human director who is responsible for supplying the necessary twigs, scrap iron, maintenance and upgrades. It might work …

We seem to have come back, courtesy of the next-best thing to a robot, to the question of whether an AI is – even for rather limited purposes – to be put on the same plane as a human. It seems so. At the end of his talk on 'Intelligent Machinery, A Heretical Theory', Alan Turing said this:

> Let us now assume, for the sake of argument, that these machines are a genuine possibility, and look at the consequences of constructing them. To do so would of course meet with great opposition, unless we have advanced greatly in religious toleration from the days of Galileo … There would be plenty to do, i.e. in trying to keep one's intelligence up to the standard set by the machines, for it seems probable that once the machine thinking method had started, it would not take long to outstrip our feeble powers. There would be no question of the machines dying, and they would be able to converse with each other to sharpen their wits. At some stage therefore we should have to expect the machines to take control, in the way that is mentioned in Samuel Butler's 'Erewhon'.

He was right to refer to *Erewhon*, but as things turned out, it would be a different feature of Butler's inverted world that forced itself into his life.

POSTBAG

It was May 2017, and it was time for a clean-up and a chuck-out. Filing cabinets half full of old stuff were prime candidates for metal and paper recycling. Fortunately for history, the chief chucker-outer was Professor Jim Miles of the School of Computer Science at Manchester University, and his eagle eye saw the words 'Alan Turing' on an orange paper file at the back of the bottom drawer of one cabinet:

> When I first found it I initially thought, 'that can't be what I think it is,' but a quick inspection showed it was a file of old letters and correspondence by Alan Turing. I was astonished such a thing had remained hidden out of sight for so long. No one who now works in the School or at the University knew they even existed.[1]

The find is the most significant and substantial addition to our knowledge of Alan Turing, and in particular the last four years of his life, since the publication of Andrew Hodges's masterly biography in 1984. Certainly, since then various collections of documents have surfaced, notably the archive of papers of

Mike Woodger (Alan Turing's colleague at the NPL) deposited in the Science Museum, and the declassification of World War Two materials relating to Bletchley Park and the development of the Delilah speech-encipherment machine have cast light in various technical areas. But the Manchester trove is different. It is the 1950s equivalent of an email file – the inbox and sent items – with all the humdrum to-and-fro of the daily round of an academic of that time. The subjects would be familiar to many professors nowadays: correspondence on theses written by PhD candidates, a request for additional secretarial staff, cover for Professor Newman while he was on sabbatical, requests from journals both learned and otherwise to contribute articles – not much has changed in seventy years. There are also innumerable requests for offprints, for in the days before cheap photocopying and online publication the offprint was the main way in which academics could keep abreast of each other's work. The last dated communication in the files[2] is from 2 June 1954, five days before Alan Turing took his own life. It is a request from Philadelphia for copies of Alan's papers on the Word Problem and Ordinal Logics.

For the first two years of Alan's time at Manchester, 1949 and 1950, the file is sparse, but there is enough to indicate his growing interest in cybernetics and morphogenesis. The study of control in robots was evolving into the balancing of forces which control the development of living things. Not surprisingly, though, the Manchester computer built by the Ferranti company features in a great deal of the correspondence: people want to come and use it, and to know whether its capabilities are up to solving their mathematical problems. Of interest are a small number of letters requiring Alan to surrender his intellectual property rights over the NPL computer – Alan Turing never made a fortune from being the 'inventor of the computer'

– not that it would have made any difference to me, since what little wealth he had would not have devolved to me anyway under the tortuous route taken under various family wills.

The 141 sets of documents in the new archive might be disappointing to some, who hope to learn of new directions for Alan Turing's work in his final years; an inbox doesn't contain that kind of thing, though. Rather, the interest is in what it tells us about Alan himself. With some correspondents he is short and businesslike:

> 9th August 1951. Dear Miller [Dr Jeffrey Miller of Cambridge University], Your statement as to what we did with the Mersenne numbers is quite correct. I had very little to do with it myself. Professor Newman made up the routine and Dr Kilburn put them through on the machine. I wonder if you have finished with my paper on Zeta Function. I should be glad to have it back fairly soon.[3]

One correspondent, a John Hill from Cardiff, wrote in 1951 asking about the logical design of the Manchester computer; one wonders what his reaction was when he received a reply referring him to Alan's paper 'On Computable Numbers'. Others get a more sympathetic handling. One is Beatrice Worsley, who had done her PhD at Cambridge under Maurice Wilkes. Her thesis is described as the first computer science doctorate and she herself as Canada's first female computer scientist (in fact, she was probably Canada's first computer scientist).[4] The correspondence between her and Alan Turing begins after she went back to Canada in late 1951:

> 9th Jan. '52. Dear Dr Turing … Bennett and Pollard, of Ferranti's, visited me last month, and gave me lots of news.

Manchester progress is most commendable, and your Mark II is highly esteemed over here. Unfortunately, Toronto is letting [the University of Toronto Electronic Computer] pass away without giving it much of a work-out. The engineers are concentrating on the design of a much more ambitious machine, which seems rather a short-sighted policy to me. They refuse to hire enough mathematicians to give them a run for their money. I am doing a piece of theoretical work for my thesis now, but plan to try some remote control work on your machine as soon as I have time. With best wishes for the new year.

17th Jan. 1952. Dear Dr. Turing:- In connection with your article 'on Computable Numbers', I am having difficulty in identifying a machine such as the Reduced Machine of the Manchester Mark II Handbook with your theoretical one … In connection with your paper on 'Computing Machinery and Intelligence', I am still trying to think of some property of the human mind which could not be duplicated by the 'imitation game'. I feel intuitively that if there is one, it must be in the direction of spontaneity. McCulloch and Pitts, in an article in the Bulletin of Mathematical Biophysics, postulate a brain mechanism in which the threshold of excitement of the neuron can be determined by the neuron itself. Since the visit of Bennett and Pollard, I have become enthused about the possibility of doing some work on the Mark II machine after completing the Cambridge Degree work. I am therefore applying for a Research Fellowship in this connection. This requires a statement from the Computing Machine Laboratory in Manchester to say that I would be enabled to use the Lab. facilities and that my work would be suitably supervised … Thank you for your continued interest.

25th January 1952. Dear Miss Worsley, I was interested in your idea of working the machine by remote control. I think it would be a most interesting experiment and I would be glad to let you do so ... We would certainly be willing to let you use the Laboratory if you succeed in obtaining a Research Fellowship, and to supervise your work.

9th Feb. 1952. Dear Dr Turing ... Your long letter is most helpful, as I usually find the simplest concepts the most difficult to accept ... I see how to derive the logical operations now, thank you. It seems that one must retain a distinction between digital manipulation and intellectual concept. You are welcome to see what I do with the subject, but it probably won't please you as it must satisfy the Cambridge palate.

19 Nov. 1952. Dear Dr Turing:- By now you will probably have heard that our new Computer, the FERUT, has passed its acceptance trials, and is working well enough to keep us more than busy ... We are all looking forward to having Miss Popplewell join us early in the new year. Some time ago, we were confronted with an integro-differential equation, and I would very much like to have some expert advice on it before we plunge into too much numerical work. The problem is that of finding the mass distribution, $f(x, t)$ of the particles in a cloud of raindrops ...

26th November 1952. Dear Miss Worsley, It is good to hear that things are getting on the move so well at Toronto ... As regards raindrops ... The whole thing seems to me to need much more thought in the physics than in the computation ... It is really rather a relief that one has to do so much more planning and theory than programming. It was certainly the same at N.P.L. The customers never really knew either what they wanted or how the computations should be done. Very often they could be satisfied with a bit of theory and no computation at all.[5]

Beatrice is relaxed enough to hint at the tensions between Alan and Maurice Wilkes, and she gets Alan out of his technical shell. I think Beatrice Worsley and Alan Turing got on rather well.

Another long series of correspondence in the files is with an American mathematician called William Boone.[6] The first piece of pure-mathematics research done by Alan after he arrived in Manchester was published under the gripping title 'The Word Problem in Semi-Groups with Cancellation' in volume 52 of the *Annals of Mathematics*. The 'word problem' seems to have grabbed Alan's attention because it's formally quite close to a problem in codebreaking. The 'word problem' is, in a sense, a challenge of encryption and decryption: you take a string of nonsensical letters and, one by one, add

A few of the Cambridge Mathematical Laboratory team, May 1949. Beatrice Worsley is seated, far right; Maurice Wilkes is seated in the centre. (© Computer Laboratory, University of Cambridge. Reproduced with permission)

on a second string of nonsense, hoping that each letter in the new string cancels out the effect of one in the first string. If the entire sequence is cancelled, you are left with the plain-text decrypt. For mathematicians, the question was whether there is an algorithm – a Turing machine, even – which can tell you up front if the process is going to be successful. (For codebreakers, it may be that this is an important question too.) The 'word problem' was posed in 1910 and hadn't been solved, but Alan Turing's paper concluded that there was no such algorithm, at least for the situations he was considering. (At this point, the codebreakers could be forgiven for wondering if there was an algorithm for deciding up front if reading the paper is worth the trouble.) On 24 July 1951, William Boone enters the lists, having found something that might be errors in Alan Turing's paper. The scene is set for one of Alan's brush-offs – except that's not how it turns out. Over the course of the next two years there is a respectful exchange of letters, warming to cordiality and, ultimately, the suggestion that Boone might come to Manchester to do postdoctoral research alongside Alan Turing. Unfortunately, he didn't get to Manchester until 1958, but he did solve the word problem completely – though, in a replay of Alan Turing's work on logic, the proof was published after that of another mathematician, so the solution is associated with P.S. Novikov rather than William W. Boone.

Perhaps the most fascinating thing about Alan Turing's postbag is that it spans the awful year 1952 when he was arrested, committed for trial, and then tried at the Knutsford Assizes for 'gross indecency'. It is fascinating because the correspondence carries on regardless of these events – there is no sense from the flow, subject matter or tone of the material that anything out of the ordinary has gone on in his life. Alan is corresponding with people about coming to use the Manchester computer, about talks on his new theory of morphogenesis, and (rather significantly) engaged in a discussion with the evolutionary biologist J.B.S. Haldane about the 'primordial soup'. Haldane was twenty years senior to Alan, and had published a famous paper in 1929 on the origins of life in the goo that possibly existed on Earth millions of years before self-reproducing life-forms emerged. Between his committal on 27 February and his trial on 31 March, Haldane is writing to Alan Turing about the number of bits needed for early genetic code, and he goes on:

> This at once raises the problem of the origin of life. In a primitive ocean of volume of about 1024ml, lasting about 109 years and probably full of miscellaneous metastable organic molecules made from NH_3 and CH_4 in absence of O_2 by solar radiation, you would have a reasonable probability of getting a self-producing system with about 100 bits of control built in, by chance, but almost none of getting one with 200 bits. As a bacteriophage is said to have about 45 genes, this is not an uninteresting figure.

Alan Turing replies, on 19 March:

> As regards self reproducing chemical systems, I am inclined to think that the most primitive systems with this property were altogether simpler than the current gene systems, and that the primitive ones have now been altogether displaced. Also that these primitive systems contain many fewer bits than anything you mention. Although there could be as you say between 2100 & 2200 experiments which could be tried out in the time and space available, I expect that really the number of different combinations that are tried is quite small. The 'winning combination' may depend on

a relatively small number of moves, but some of them may be relatively unlikely ones, because they involve crossing a rather high energy barrier.[7]

The origin of life was a game of chess, or at least could be seen through the lens of Game Theory. That subject was a creature of John von Neumann, who once upon a time had offered Alan a job at Princeton and whose many, many novel concepts and ideas included the logic plan for all post-war computing machines: that, the *First Draft of a Report on the EDVAC*, came into Alan Turing's hands in 1945 and was highly influential in his own design of the ACE at the NPL. Alan's trial was itself another exercise in Game Theory, with a number of possible moves, and a dystopian rulebook. Moral choices would be made, probably by other players. Richard Braithwaite, Alan's philosopher friend from King's College, Cambridge, mused that ethics itself might be a branch of Game Theory, in one letter in the Manchester archive.[8] Alan's future was going to be the outcome of a game.

The problem was this: if you were gay, you were presumably bad, for homosexual activity between men was a criminal offence. But theory of criminology holds that if you are not in control of yourself, you might be insane, and therefore not guilty but, rather, to be treated with compassion as a patient. Most of the gay men tried at the Knutsford Assizes on the same day as Alan Turing were treated as being bad, and fined or sent to prison; Alan alone was treated as being mad, and sent off for 'treatment'. In this upside-down world, taken straight out of Samuel Butler's *Erewhon* (where crime is treated as if it were a disease, but illness is punishable), the question was what 'treatment' Alan Turing should receive for his 'illness'. No problem of diagnosis is too challenging for a psychiatrist, and it was readily apparent that Alan Turing was suffering from something called homosexuality. Which was a crime, and not something that should be treated, but something which should be punished. Except ...

It was an uncomputable paradox, exactly the sort of conundrum which had allowed Gödel to prove that there were unsolvable problems and Turing to prove that it was impossible to say whether a problem was solvable or not. It would be gloriously amusing if it really were a game, or if it were happening to someone else – and yet Alan Turing coped with it all admirably, even defiantly.

I do not intend to defend the witch-doctoring which passed for mental health science in the early 1950s, or the consequences for Alan once he had fallen into its clutches. He was at least blessed with a human being for a psychiatrist, even though the Manchester Royal Infirmary took it upon itself to inflict torture in the form of hormone injections and a hormone implant. From these facts we are left with a picture of an evil state which actually drove Alan Turing towards suicide, causing mental illness where it was supposed to be 'curing' it.

Consider the scene from towards the end of *The Imitation Game*, the feature film about Alan Turing and Bletchley Park released in 2014. Alan is explaining the consequences of his trial to Joan Clarke. He drops a glass of water and explains why he is undergoing hormone 'therapy':

JOAN CLARKE	Your hands ... You're twitching.
ALAN TURING	No I'm not.
[He is.]	
JOAN CLARKE	Alan.
ALAN TURING	... It's the medication.
JOAN CLARKE	The medication?

ALAN TURING	I have to go in for weekly oestrogen treatments. At the hospital.
JOAN CLARKE	What are you talking about?
ALAN TURING	The judge gave me a choice. Prison. Or 'hormonal therapy.'
JOAN CLARKE	Oh my god. Oh my god. That's—
ALAN TURING	—Chemical castration. Yes. To cure my homosexual predilections. Of course I chose that. I wouldn't be able to work from prison.

[Joan is HORRIFIED.]

| ALAN TURING | Well how would I even have got parts in jail? It just makes no sense. |

Alan Turing has, apparently, chosen the therapy in order to work on his computing machine, idiotically named 'Christopher', which is (even more idiotically) located in his front room. In the screenplay, he is clearly portrayed as an obsessive monomaniac.

But this interpretation of Alan Turing's trial is just plain wrong. Even if you strip out the idiotic nonsense from the movie, the impression which is left about Alan Turing's trial is of mistreatment at the hands of the British Establishment. Many people have been profoundly moved by this story, portrayed in this way. Unfortunately, it is, if not entirely nonsense, close to a distortion, happily fostered by moviemakers who can sniff out a good plot. The British Establishment did not hang Alan Turing out to dry. To start with, his ex-colleague Hugh Alexander from Bletchley Park, by 1952 a senior official at GCHQ, came to speak for his defence. His testimony explained – without giving away any secrets – how significant Alan's wartime contribution had been. And Alan's professor at

Manchester, M.H.A. Newman, described Alan's groundbreaking work on the 'electronic brain' and the importance of his research for British prestige. The legal team had a plan: using the intervention of these two character witnesses they were able to lead the judge towards the possibility of probation, treating Alan Turing as mad rather than bad – a ploy to stop Alan going to prison, getting a formal criminal record, and losing his post at Manchester University. So far from being abandoned, he was being given the best support possible.

Nevertheless, something – quite apart from the absurdities of his 'treatment' – had gone amiss in the Alan Turing case. The question has to be asked why (apart from his own foolishness in telling the police that the identity of his burglar was an acquaintance of a male visitor) Alan was in court at all. The answer may be that Alan Turing was, in a small way, something of a minor celebrity because of his 'artificial brain', which was in the papers and on the BBC and at the centre of the debate over whether machines can think. The police had caught a biggish fish, which would make them look good. In the handful of other 'gross indecency' cases being tried at the March 1952 Knutsford Assizes there was only one count on the indictment, but in Alan's case there were six counts each against him and against his partner. I can't explain that other than that the police were, in some sense, out to get him.

Let us return to the question of Alan Turing and mental illness. Consider this scene:

[YOUNG ALAN TURING, 15, sits alone in the dining hall. Other BOYS joke and laugh and tell animated stories at nearby tables, but Alan sits alone, staring intently at his food. ON ALAN'S PLATE: Boiled steak. Potatoes. Peas. And carrots.]

ALAN TURING [voiceover]: Carrots are orange. Peas are
green. They mustn't touch.
[Alan carefully tries to separate the carrots from the peas. It's
like he's performing brain surgery.]

The next thing that happens in the movie is that some other
boys tip a whole load of vegetables over Alan, and he is left
squealing, 'Carrots are orange! Carrots are orange! Carrots
are orange!' This scene comes from the imagination of the
screenwriter, since I can't find anything in Andrew Hodges's
biography, or Alan's letters home, or anywhere else actually,
to justify it. Sure, Alan Turing had to undergo the 'robust'
environment of a British boarding school in the 1920s, and
none of us would much like our own children to have to go
through that. But his letters home describe it with a sort of
wryness which indicate that he was not being singled out, and
– as with his 'treatment' at the hands of the medical profession
thirty years later – he could cope with this sort of thing as well
as anyone else.

Evidently, the screenwriter of *The Imitation Game* had got
the idea, from somewhere, that Alan Turing was on the autism
spectrum. The verdict of 1952 was obviously not good enough:
since the release of the movie, Alan Turing has been on public
trial – this time, it seems, he is accused (in the manner of
Erewhon) of having autism or Asperger's syndrome.

One might imagine that a brilliant mathematician like Alan
Turing had astonishing powers of mental arithmetic. Alan's
fellow codebreaker Alexander Aitken, from Hut 6 at Bletchley,
might have qualified on that score:

Professor Aitken's students tell many stories of the prodigious ability in mental arithmetic which he demonstrates

in his lectures . For example, Professor Aitken was once asked to multiply 123456789 by 987654321; he immediately remarked to himself that 987654321 is 80000000001/81, thereby converting a tedious sum into a 'gift.' ... Even as a schoolboy he was able to astonish his fellows by squaring 57586 in his head in two seconds.

This comes from *Faster than Thought*, that little book about computers – in this case a human computer – which Ferranti's put out to boost their machine.[9] However, Alan Turing was himself a 'lousy computer', according to his NPL colleague J.H. Wilkinson, and it's no surprise that the Manchester Archive includes several requests for details and orders for mechanical calculators for Alan Turing's personal use.[10] To see

Alan Turing's 'Britannic' calculator from his time at Manchester. (By kind permission of the University of Manchester/Jim Miles)

if Alan Turing was on the autism spectrum, we shall have to look for other evidence.

A few years before *The Imitation Game* screenplay was written, a piece appeared in the *Irish Journal of Psychiatric Medicine* under the title 'Did Alan Turing have Asperger's syndrome?'[11] The learned authors of the piece weighed up the evidence, and pronounced Alan Turing guilty. Unfortunately, in the pages of this particular journal, the evidence is not tested by cross-examination, and some of the facts put forward to make the case for the prosecution are not honoured with a reference, so we can't check the sources and do that for ourselves. In fact, the evidence is about as unscientifically compiled as that which led to Alan being treated for a 'mental condition' in 1952. Let me try and have a go, though.

- Under the heading 'imposition of routines and interests on himself and others', we find that Alan '*always* ate an apple before going to bed'; and '*invariably* mulled a bottle of wine for dinner and *always* put the cork back in the bottle' [my emphasis]. My grandmother – not a very reliable witness, particularly when you recall that Alan Turing lived alone for the whole of his adult life – said he sometimes had an apple at night (famously, he used one to disguise the taste of the cyanide he ate at the time of his death). To me it seems a bit strange to diagnose someone as having Asperger's on the grounds that they recork their wine. Where the alwayses and invariablys come from is not explained.

- Alan 'certainly imposed his interests on others'. The evidence here is that he wrote to his mother about science and to Christopher Morcom's mother about 'the nature of spirit'. Since Mother wanted to hear about science, and Mother wanted Alan (an atheist) to write to Christopher's mother about religion, I suggest this hardly shows him imposing his interests on others. It might have been more convincing if the writers had discussed how Alan coped with everyday conversation about non-technical stuff – my father said that 'Alan could not stand social chat or what he was pleased to call "vapid conversation"'[12] – but they don't mention this.

• We get fewer adverbs under the headings 'Non-verbal communication problems', 'Speech and language problems' and 'Severe impairment in reciprocal social interaction'. Let's set aside the inconvenient fact that the BBC asked Alan to do not just one but three radio shows, since there is a case to answer here. Lyn Irvine, who was M.H.A. Newman's wife and knew Alan very well indeed, said that Alan had a strange way of not meeting the eyes, and of sidling out of the door with a brusque and offhand manner. I could add that Jerry Roberts, who worked with Alan at Bletchley Park, has a similar description of Alan's behaviour;[13] so did the Americans he worked with, who complained of his lack of hail-fellow-well-met sociability which is so vital in American politeness; and my own father remembered Alan's ill-bred behaviour at a cocktail party – and the fact that he remembered it some thirty years later almost certainly means that my father was incensed at the time. (You didn't want to be around John Turing when he was furious, by the way.) To this charge sheet we must also add that Alan Turing had a stammer; according to Alan's friend and colleague I.J. Good, 'In discussions he was excitable, and his voice would rise to a high pitch, although he was not in the least quarrelsome. Between sentences he had a habit of saying "Ah-ah-ah-ah-ah …" which made it difficult to interrupt his line of thought, or even to have a line of thought of one's own!'[14] But, whether these things are 'problems' or 'severe impairment' is a question of degree, and ultimately one for the person on the receiving end.

• Finally, the authors address the count of: 'An all-absorbing narrow interest that includes exclusion of other activities, repetitive adherence, more rote than meaning.' To ascribe any of this to Alan Turing, whose interests and achievements ranged from ground-breaking discoveries in pure mathematics, codebreaking, computer science, technological design, cybernetics and developmental biology, seems bizarre in the extreme. Needless to say, the evidence put forward by the authors is completely unconvincing.

While the verdict of these authors is, therefore, open to challenge, it is dated and perhaps shouldn't be taken too seriously. Like a great deal of understanding about mental health, the description of Asperger's syndrome has evolved over the years and has now been merged into the wider diagnosis of autism spectrum disorder. These days, the diagnostic criteria are 'persistent difficulties with social communication and social interaction' and 'restricted and repetitive patterns of behaviours, activities or interests' which may 'limit and impair everyday functioning'. Personally, I don't recognise Alan Turing in these phrases.

The UK's National Autistic Society has helpful advice and guidance for those who may have a child with these difficulties. Their efforts to improve diagnosis and steer the way that unimpaired people interact with those on the spectrum away from alarm and disengagement are to be applauded. Perhaps those experiencing the condition in one way or another are looking for a historical role model, but I struggle to see how one could be found in the case of Alan Turing. All we can say is that the studies of Kanner and Asperger, the two child psychiatrists who first described ASD in the 1940s, came to wider attention long after Alan Turing was dead. Nobody was diagnosing Alan Turing against ASD criteria in 1952, or at any other stage in his lifetime. Dr Greenbaum, Alan Turing's own psychiatrist, didn't find anything much 'wrong' with him in the 1950s. Alan Turing was intellectual, uncomfortable in middle-class social settings, and gay; the last of these led to him being placed in the hands of the shrinks, and it is more of a commentary on our own times than his that the story of Alan Turing is still a playground for psychologists. I suspect that the problem, if there still is one, is that Alan Turing was more brilliant than us, so we need to put him in a box duly labelled with a pathology so we can feel better about our meagre selves. If so, not a lot has changed since 1952.

Back in the 1950s, though, it was a social stigma to be homosexual as much as to be mentally ill, exaggerated by the inability to distinguish the one from the other. Writing about it all after twenty-five years, my father wrote, 'I had never had even the faintest notion that Alan was a homosexual. One did not in those days (at least in our middle class) talk or even think about homosexuals and lesbians.' He was being soft on himself, having moved a little bit with the times. Back in the 1950s, it was different. John's eldest daughter recalled in 2013 that she had been at boarding school in the spring of 1952, and received an unexpected visit from her parents. 'Daddy said to me, "If anyone asks you if Alan is your uncle, say, 'No, I don't know him.'" I didn't understand and Daddy didn't explain. It was only later that I realised what lay behind it.'[15] Alan's conviction, and more importantly his sexuality, was something that needed to be covered up.

Turing family relations weren't exactly easy, especially after the exposé of 1952. Alan had brought the whole thing down on himself, by reporting a break-in, which had been the indirect consequence of Alan's relationship with his co-defendant Arnold Murray. John (my father) wrote:

Alan did not seem to understand, even then, how close he had been to disaster, though did he, I wonder, have some premonition of things to come? He continued to talk about 'the burglar' and wrote me an unpleasant letter suggesting that I cared nothing for his plight or that of homosexuals in general (the latter, perhaps, being not far wide of the mark) and that I was merely concerned to protect myself and my partners from adverse comment in the City from our Establishment friends. It was so far from the truth that I sent him a tart reply of which I feel ashamed. It was a disagreeable business and the only occasion I can remember that we quarrelled.

As for Alan's mother:

My mother was fully aware of it [Alan's sexuality] before Alan's death (not, I imagine, that she had the faintest idea of what it implied), but she makes no reference to it in her book. One can put that down to Edwardian reticence if one pleases. In my view, based on such conversation as I had with my mother about it, necessarily reduced to a minimum, her reaction was much what one might expect if a specialist had informed her that her son was colour-blind or had an incurable obsession with spiders: it was a nasty shock of brief duration and of no great significance.

Actually, she might have known more than John perceived; if he's right about her reaction, it is commendably out of alignment with mainstream values of the early 1950s. Here is Alan, writing to his friend P.N. Furbank, in 1953:

July 12. Mother has been staying here, and we seem to be getting on a good deal better. I have been subjecting her to a good deal of sexual enlightenment and she seems to have stood up to it very well. There was a rather absurd dream I had the other night in which I asked mother's opinion about going to bed with some men and she said 'O very well, but don't going walking about the place naked, like you did before'.[16]

There is also another letter, and another cover-up. In 1954, Mother received a letter of condolence from C.H.O'D Alexander, Alan's colleague from Bletchley Park whose evidence swung the judge away from a criminal sentence in 1952. Mother put the letter into the archive of Alan's papers at King's College, Cambridge, but not before she had overwritten much of the first page to make it illegible. Shortly before Christmas 2020, with the aid of spectroscopic imaging and some latter-day codebreaking, the things that my grandmother wanted concealed have been brought to light. The covered-over words seem to say:

I very well remember at the time of his trouble 2 years ago that what alarmed both Newman and myself more than anything else was that he would be asked if he admitted that what he had done was morally wrong. Rightly or wrongly he himself did not think he had done wrong and that being so he would rather have been imprisoned than admit to it; and it wasn't obstinacy, he just would not have lied in order to escape.[17]

We shall probably never know whether it was the painful episode of the trial, the question of guilt or her son's position on the morality of sexual preference that Sara Turing most wanted to hide. She also deleted the word 'psychoanalytic' from the same letter, where it referred to the therapy Alan was receiving. Clearly Sara saw all these things as shameful, best kept out of sight.

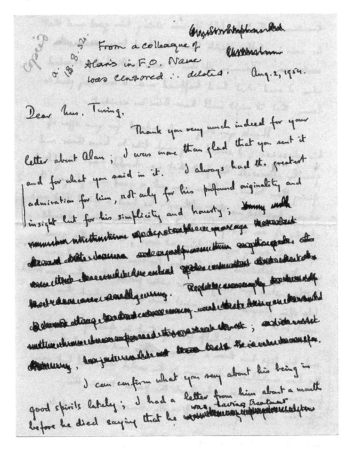

Alexander's redacted letter to Sara Turing. (Reproduced with kind permission of the Provost and Scholars of King's College, Cambridge)

In wider circles, the stigma, or the fear of it, endured for decades. Andrew Hodges, who began work on the first fully comprehensive biography of Alan Turing in the late 1970s, told me that even then the academic community was enthused by his idea of a Turing biography – provided that he left out the awkward fact of Alan's sexuality. Andrew, quite rightly, rejected the advice.

In 1952, the strategy of covering up Alan's sexuality with the blanket of Service to the Nation, coupled with the probation ruse suggested by the lawyers in Knutsford, worked. The judge 'bound over' Alan for a year and sent him off to the Manchester Royal Infirmary for 'treatment'. Alan returned to his job and his correspondence file picks up again within a few days, as if nothing has happened. It doesn't reveal that, in secret, Alan had been doing some consulting work for GCHQ after the war; he learned in the autumn of 1952 that the climate of mistrust which had built up following the Maclean and Burgess spy scandals (they defected in 1951) now precluded anyone who was a known homosexual having clearance for this work.[18] They must have put this gently to him, for he seems to have accepted the news in good spirit; and there is friendly correspondence dating from November 1952 with the new head of GCHQ, also a veteran of Bletchley Park, about providing a photo of Alan for a 'rogues' gallery' (Alan's phrase[19]) being compiled by William F. Friedman, the chief American cryptanalyst.

Apart from this branding of gay people as security risks, officialdom seems to have been unconcerned about Alan's conviction. In November, Alan Turing was invited by the Foreign Office – notionally his old department from the war years – to participate in a lecture tour of Germany, being arranged for 'university teachers of standing'. The Manchester correspondence file shows that he accepted, and applied to the vice chancellor of the university for leave of absence to make the tour.[20]

On 22 January 1953, though, things suddenly changed. To the university registrar he writes: 'Thank you for letting me know about the permission to lecture in Germany. I have however now cancelled my tour, as I found myself unable to undertake the work that would be involved.' To his friend and NPL ex-colleague E.T. Goodwin, he writes, 'On second thoughts … I should really be quite glad not to lecture at this conference' – only the day after he writes accepting an invitation to speak at the NPL's Symposium on Automatic Digital Computation. And to Donald MacKay he rejects an invitation to another symposium, this one being organised by Warren McCulloch, the American professor at MIT who had shown that a Turing machine could be realised in a network of neurons, and was now doing pioneering work on neural networks – if anything was up Alan's street, this was it. 'Although the meetings themselves would appeal to me, I would very much prefer not to go. I would not like the journey, and I detest America: furthermore I do not wish to ask for leave of absence from the University.'[21]

This is extraordinary, a complete turnaround of his mood, and the outburst about 'detesting' America is absurd. Donald MacKay had perhaps encouraged the xenophobia, for in his own letter MacKay seems to need to excuse the Americans. ('They're a good bunch – as Warren says, friendly people, full of idle curiosity, & eager to know what you'll have to say, however rude in their shirt sleeves!') But 'detest America'? This is out of character: Alan's letter of 19 October 1951 declining an invitation to take up a Visiting Professorship at MIT seems to indicate a genuine reluctance.[22] (Sure, there were some things which grated against British opinion of proper cultural values; to take one example, William F. Friedman's natty bow tie and two-tone shoes would be thought vulgar in Britain, even to someone as badly dressed as Alan. In Britain, two-colour shoes were 'co-respondent' shoes, worn by disreputable witnesses hired for the day to 'prove' adultery in consensual divorce proceedings.)

Something bad had happened to Alan Turing.

A clue is given in a letter to Alan's best friend from Hanslope Park, Robin Gandy, who later went on to be editor of Alan's collected works and contributed his own archive of original correspondence and other papers connected with Alan to the collection at King's College, Cambridge.[23] In typical Alan Turing fashion, this letter was printed out by the Manchester computer; you have to understand that a computer couldn't just be set up with a word-processing app in 1953, so it was something of a feat to get the machine to behave like a typewriter. Alan is apologising for not attending to Robin's ideas about the 'theory of perception': 'YOUR LAST LETTER ARRIVED IN THE MIDDLE OF A CRISIS ABOUT "DEN NORSKE GUTT"'. *Den norske Gutt* – the Norwegian youth – was a young man called Kjell, with whom Alan had become smitten on a holiday in Norway the previous summer. Alan's computer routines had thereafter been named after Kjell, and it seems that Kjell had agreed to come to Britain to spend some time with Alan. On 11 March, Alan was composed enough to write to Robin Gandy about it more fully, this time using an actual pen (though, in Alan fashion, the reverse side of the letter is covered with equations, with a line through the lot of them):

> The Kjell crisis has now evaporated. It was very active for about a week. It started by my getting a P.C. [postcard] from

him saying he was on his way to visit me. At one stage police over the N of England were out searching for him, especially in Wilmslow, Manchester, Newcastle etc. I will tell you all one day. He is now back in Bergen without my even seeing him! For sheer incident it almost rivals the Arnold story.

The 'Arnold story' is, of course, the tale which led to Alan's conviction the previous year. At this distance of time it is impossible to get to the bottom of what happened in 1953: how the police could have made a connection that led to – apparently – them turning up at Alan's home in Wilmslow, hoping to catch him red-handed. It may be no coincidence that Alan's probation did not expire until April 1953. With only weeks of good behaviour still to go, Alan's life was completely up-ended.

The correspondence file in Manchester cannot provide a complete answer to our questions. But the contrast between Alan's calm dismissal of what happened in the spring of 1952 and his wildly disrupted behaviour of January 1953 is telling. We can certainly see that there were far more things going on in Alan Turing's life than we presently understand. Before I looked into the matter properly, like many people I had assumed that 'legal persecution drove Turing to take his own life', to quote one newspaper report from 2009.[24] Now I think differently, but the imagined link between Alan Turing's trial, treatment and death remains so powerful a force on the public imagination that we should take a closer look at it.

APPLE

The death of Alan Turing, a year after the Kjell crisis of 1953, has an enduring popular fascination. It came as a shock to his friends and his family, and I am constantly asked what I make of it. There were no obvious forewarnings: Robin Gandy, Alan's friend, had stayed over the previous weekend and 'they seemed to have a really good time', according to Mrs Clayton, Alan's housekeeper.[1] Nor is there much in the way of evidence about the weekend of his death. George Gibson, a neighbour, gave testimony at the inquest:

> During Sunday 6th June, 1954, I was at the front of my residence near the garage doors, and on looking across my front garden towards Adlington Road, I noticed the man, whom I know to be Mr Turing of 'Hollymeade' Adlington Road, Wilmslow, walking along Adlington Road towards the direction of Wilmslow … When I saw Mr Turing on the Sunday morning he was dressed in a grey sleeveless pullover, and in his shirt sleeves. He was not wearing a hat. I have often seen Mr. Turing about the district, and as usual he looked very dishevelled.

Mr Gibson may have been the last person to see Alan alive. Mrs Clayton came in on Mondays, Tuesdays, Thursdays and Fridays in the evening to clean and make his dinner. Monday, 7 June was a bank holiday, so Mrs Clayton didn't come in that day. The next day, she arrived just before 5 p.m.:

> I had been away for the weekend and went up tonight as usual to get his meal. Saw his bedroom light on, the lounge curtains not drawn back, milk on steps & paper in door. So I thought he'd gone out early & forgot to put his light off so I went & knocked at his bedroom door. Got no answer so walked in. Saw him in bed he must have died during the night.
>
> I saw Mr Turing lying in bed. The bed clothes were up to his face. I saw what appeared to be froth all round his mouth. He was on his back and appeared to be dead. I touched his hand which was cold. I went immediately to a nearby house and caused the Police to be informed.

The policeman, Sergeant Cottrell, described the scene as well:

> I examined the body and found no signs of life. The body was cold and the limbs were stiff. The deceased was lying on his back, in practically a normal position on the bed. His right arm was bent inwards at the elbow and projecting over the side of the bed. His left arm was also bent at the elbow with the hand resting on the stomach. The bed clothes were pulled up towards the chest and neck part of the deceased. The deceased was dressed in pyjamas. I noticed a white frothy liquid about the mouth towards the left side and cheek. There was no [sign] of burning about the [mouth], but there was a faint smell of bitter almonds about the

mouth. I examined the external parts of the body and there were no marks of violence or any other injury to the body. On the small table at the side of the bed, on the right side, I noticed a half slice of apple. Several bites had been taken from the side of this piece of apple.

The final piece of evidence was given by a pathologist, Dr Bird:

> On instructions from H.M. Coroner I performed a post mortem examination on the body identified to me as that of Alan Mathison Turing … The examination was at the Public Mortuary Wilmslow at 8 p.m. Tuesday 8th June, 1954. I produce the report of my findings … I also removed at the time of examination the stomach and duodenum and contents, and some blood from the deceased, and the next day tested these chemically and found cyanide present. On the evening of 8th June 1954 I had been with Police Officers when a search of the house was made, and a jam jar 1lb size of cyanide solution was found in the back room of the first floor. Electrolytic apparatus of a sort was rigged up in that room and was connected with the electric light pendant from the ceiling. There was a smell of cyanide in the room. In addition a bottle containing solid Potassium Cyanide was found in a drawer in the bedroom next to where the deceased was lying. In my opinion the cause of death was Asphyxia, due to Cyanide poisoning, and death was not a natural one.

The autopsy report does not contain any quantitative data on the amount of cyanide in Alan's system, but Dr Bird noted on the standard pro forma post-mortem report that many organs were reddened by the poison, smelled of bitter almonds, or both: the brain, lungs, heart and blood vessels, stomach, spleen and kidneys. It only takes 1.52 milligrams of cyanide per kilo of body weight to kill an average person,[2] and Alan had buckets of the stuff around. Not surprisingly, the coroner concluded that Alan had taken his own life.

There was no suicide note, but that wouldn't have been Alan's style, and in any case only around 30 per cent of those who take their own lives actually leave one.[3] The absence of a note, the speed at which the post-mortem and inquest took place, and the pro forma nature of the post-mortem report have all encouraged a variety of alternative theories to emerge.

Until after my grandmother died in 1976, there was no discussion of any of this at home; but then my father felt at liberty to write about his mother, her biography of Alan, and his recollection of the days after Alan's death. He even tape-recorded his thoughts. John's mission was to rebalance the story of Alan Turing's life: when he was writing, the only published biography was the hagiographic account by – who else – Sara Turing, formerly Ethel Stoney, Alan Turing's mother. And Sara firmly believed that Alan's death was no suicide but an accident. Her thinking may have been influenced subconsciously by her own religious beliefs, towards the Catholic end of the Anglican spectrum, where suicide is sinful (and therefore unthinkable in her son); and there was just enough ambiguity in the evidence to prop up her theory. She reckoned that the cyanide was in Alan's 'nightmare room' (his home laboratory) because he had been gold-plating teaspoons.

In 1976, this is what John had to say:[4]

Some two years later, during the Whitsun holiday, I had taken one of my daughters to the cinema and arrived home about 10.30 p.m. In my absence the Manchester police had telephoned to say that Alan had been found dead in his house.

Late as it was I telephoned to the ever kindly and shrewd Mr G. [a reference to Dr Greenbaum, Alan's psychiatrist], who promised to meet me at the station in Manchester the next morning. He took me to the police and thence we went to the mortuary where I identified Alan's body. He had taken cyanide. By great good fortune my mother was on holiday in Italy and did not return home until after the inquest.

Mr G. advised me strongly not to instruct Counsel to appear at the inquest and told me of the unhappy course which some other cases had taken before this coroner, a retired doctor who could not abide lawyers. The possibility of establishing death by accident was minimal; the best we could hope for was the considerate verdict of 'balance of mind disturbed'. He was right and I accepted his advice. At the inquest itself this soon became apparent: there were present some eight or nine reporters, some from the national press, with pencils poised and waiting for the homosexual revelations. They were disappointed. I gave evidence briefly. The coroner asked me a few perfunctory questions. The verdict was as anticipated.

Let me insert an editorial thought here. Publicity, in the awful circumstances, could only have spread the distress more widely. As it was, the newspapers carried a good deal of non-sense, likely to have caused quite enough grief. The thought of making it more controversial, by taking some lawyer's points about the possibility of it being an accident, would not have helped in the least.

When my mother returned she was highly indignant and made no secret of her belief that I had grossly mishandled the case. She evolved various theories of her own to establish to

SCIENTIST
(robot brain man)
IS FOUND
DEAD

Express Staff Reporter

DR Alan Mathison Turing, 41-year-old mathematics expert who worked on a mechanical brain, has been found dead at his home in Adlington-road, Wilmslow.

There will be an inquest today.

Dr Turing fed Manchester University's £100,000 "electronic brain" with intricate problems.

He once said it had solved in a few weeks a problem in higher mathematics that had been a puzzle since the eighteenth century.

It can do more arithmetic in one day than the average man can do in a lifetime—with less likelihood of making a mistake.

A Cambridge graduate, Dr Turing left the Foreign Office in 1945 to work at the National Physical Laboratory, Teddington. He was appointed Reader in

DR TURING
He fed the "brain"

Mathematics at Manchester University in 1948.

He was elected a fellow of the Royal Society in 1951.

He was a keen long-distance runner and played chess with the precision of his computing machine.

Dr Turing was unmarried.

Press report of Alan Turing's inquest.

her own satisfaction that it was really an accident. But I had worked on the very same theories myself in Manchester for nearly three days and there was one fatal flaw in them. This was the half-eaten apple beside Alan's bed where his body was found. The apple was to disguise the bitter taste of the cyanide and thus ensure that the poison would do its work.

Alan's relationship with his mother was not all it might have seemed on the surface; especially in her grief and self-analysis as a parent, she was not an objective witness. Things were worse than she knew:

In those unhappy days in Manchester [John continues] I visited Alan's psychiatrist who told me a great deal about Alan that I did not know before – among other things that he loathed his mother. I refused to believe it. He then handed me two exercise books in which Alan had entered such matters as psychiatrists require of their patients, including their dreams. 'You had better take them away and read them,' he said, adding that there was a third book, probably in Alan's house.

I viewed the two books in my hotel with horror but I was still bent on proving the accident theory and decided I had better read them. I wish I had not. Alan had been a practising homosexual since the age of puberty. His comments on his mother were scarifying. To my great relief I was mentioned only once or twice and not in opprobrious terms. I returned the books to the psychiatrist the following day.

There remained the problem of the third book for it was essential that it should be found so that it would not fall into my mother's hands. Eventually it was found and returned to the psychiatrist. Two days later my mother arrived in

Manchester and ransacked the house for clues bearing on her preconceived theories; I need hardly add that she remained unaware of the books and of Alan's feelings about her until the day of her death.

Where am I on all this? I can only look at the evidence, as can anyone else: the key documents are all publicly viewable in the online archive at King's College, Cambridge. My father's own account is not that of a dispassionate outside observer, either: his own contemporary correspondence file is also in the King's College archive, and it shows plainly enough that he marshalled Dr Greenbaum, Professor Newman, and even the undertaker to pander to the 'accident theory' when talking to Sara, to console Sara on her loss, as a coping strategy in those dark days of 1954. Whatever their own private thoughts, they were to keep them hidden. The ploy worked, but the record was written by Sara, and ever since her book was published in 1959 the primary account of Alan's death has been one which cast doubt on the inquest verdict. I myself find no flaw in that verdict. These days one would expect a toxicology report to contain some numbers which might indicate a concentration of cyanide in the system which could rule out accident or suicide more plainly. But that need not undermine the verdict, or the process undertaken in 1954. The coroner was a doctor and the pathologist was duly qualified and had visited the scene. Nobody then thought it was anything other than a case of suicide, and looking back sadly the people like Robin Gandy, who knew Alan best, said nothing different to Andrew Hodges when he interviewed them for his masterly, thorough biography twenty years later.

Suicide plays well with the standard narrative that Alan Turing took his own life because of his mistreatment at the hands of the state. While it will now be clear that I don't subscribe to that line of causation, I cannot pinpoint a more convincing alternative story. We just don't know enough about Alan Turing's state of mind in the last week of his life to be sure, and there is no external evidence. My best guess is that there may have been boyfriend trouble, but that's an extrapolation drawn from the limited evidence in my father's correspondence file at King's College.

The big problem with the theory that Alan was the victim of state brutality is that it portrays him as victim and martyr. Each of these is an unattractive persona; but whether they are attractive or not, I don't find victimhood or martyrdom in Alan Turing's make-up. His handling of the trial in 1952 was defiant and his acceptance of the hormone treatment stoic. He responded well to the sessions with his non-judgemental psychiatrist Dr Greenbaum. Finally, nobody was expecting him to take his life on that wet bank holiday weekend in June 1954. Alan was free, in control of his destiny, not frightened of death, in line with the Erewhonian philosophy which seemed to govern his world. If we claim to honour Alan Turing as victim and martyr, we do him dishonour. It is not for his death, or a dubious narrative which 'blames' some external agency for it, that he should be remembered.

Another case of the narrative overpowering the truth is the case of the apple, another symbol of Alan Turing's untimely death. Andrew Hodges's book about Alan Turing describes how, when the Walt Disney animation *Snow White and the Seven Dwarfs* came to Cambridge in 1938, Alan had been fascinated by the scene where the witch dangles an apple into a brew of 'sleeping death' – but surely the whole point of that film is that the brew does not kill Snow White but just puts her to sleep until she can be woken up by Prince Charming. I think the Alan-and-the-apple story can be a bit overblown; for once, my father may have been right. The apple at Alan's bedside was to disguise the taste of the cyanide, and the fact that it was there, and half-eaten, is powerful evidence that Alan was working to get as much of the poison into his system as he could.

The apple by the bedside resonates with computer scientists because of the famous Apple corporation logo. The logo shows an apple with a bite taken out of the side, and in earlier versions the apple had horizontal rainbow stripes. People like to imagine that the logo cleverly melds the computer's brand name with the progenitor of computing and the rainbow colours of the Pride movement. If anyone had got hold of a copy of my grandmother's book when the logo was designed in 1977, they could have read her description of Alan's death: 'No poison was found in his bedroom. There was just a partly eaten apple on the table by his bed, for, as a rule, he used to eat an apple at night.' The original edition of her book has always been something of a rarity, and even if it was available to Apple Inc. in 1977, the origin of the logo is a bit more pedestrian: in a 2009 interview, the logo's designer, Rob Janoff, said, 'When I explain the real reason why I did the bite it's kind of a let down. But I'll tell you. I designed it with a bite for scale, so people get that it was an apple not a cherry.'[5]

That was 1977, and hardly anyone (and apparently not Rob Janoff) had heard of Alan Turing. That was still broadly true in 2009, when Alan Turing's name was known mainly in mathematical, computer science and codebreaking circles. But he had a few powerful and well-known champions in other fields, notably Stephen Fry – a great supporter, incidentally, of Bletchley Park – who tweeted about Alan on 23 June 2009, which would have been his 97th birthday. The tweet was picked up by the computer scientist John Graham-Cumming, who works in cybersecurity. He said that the treatment meted out to Alan Turing 'made his blood boil', and he started an online petition to have the government apologise for it.[6] In his blog post for the day, he wrote this:

> Turing's death should remind us how prejudice ruins and degrades. Alan Turing was gay. And he was prosecuted for 'indecent acts' and eventually took his own life aged 41. This man, younger than me, killed himself because at the time homosexuality was illegal and having been prosecuted he was chemically castrated in an attempt to 'cure' him. He had been stripped of his security clearance.
>
> For years, his legacy was largely ignored outside the computer community. To quote Wikipedia: 'In 1994 a stretch of the A6010 road (the Manchester city intermediate ring road) was named Alan Turing Way. A bridge carrying this road was widened, and carries the name "Alan Turing Bridge". A frikkin' Ring Road!
>
> Isn't it time the British Government apologized for the way he was treated? We shouldn't let this anniversary of his death go by without recognizing the great works this man did and the ignominious way in which he was treated.

My reaction to the ring road was similar, if not quite as polite, although I thought that Alan himself would have found the idea of a ring road being named after him quite the funniest thing imaginable.

The outcome was – with over 30,000 signatures, including that of Stephen Fry – that the petition hit its mark. Prime Minister Gordon Brown phoned John Graham-Cumming, and the government issued an official apology, which includes the following paragraph:

Thousands of people have come together to demand justice for Alan Turing and recognition of the appalling way he was treated. While Turing was dealt with under the law of the time, and we can't put the clock back, his treatment was of course utterly unfair, and I am pleased to have the chance to say how deeply sorry I and we all are for what happened to him. Alan and the many thousands of other gay men who were convicted, as he was convicted, under homophobic laws, were treated terribly.

That was certainly more elegant and gracious than a ring road.

The apology was soon followed by 2012, the centenary year of Alan Turing's birth, marked by a worldwide celebration mostly in academic circles but also with theatrical, musical, artistic and other contributions. It was a year when the eyes of the world were turned to the UK, with the Olympic Games held in London and Queen Elizabeth's golden jubilee, so it is perhaps not surprising that the new government which had taken office since the date of the apology decided to arrange for a royal pardon for Alan.

This, I have to say, was something I found much more difficult to rationalise than the apology. In the first place, as Gordon Brown's statement said, Alan Turing was dealt with under the law of the time, and we can't put the clock back. Alan Turing was by no means the only person to be convicted under Section 11 of the Criminal Law Amendment Act 1885. Apparently almost 50,000 men suffered under this law, some of whom were celebrities; more were convicted under similar anti-gay legislation. Oscar Wilde is the most famous victim, apart from Alan Turing, but the 1950s attitude to prosecution, if not persecution, of gay men perhaps deserves retelling. The MP and writer H. Montgomery Hyde spelt out the unfairness of it all in a book published shortly after the eventual relaxation of Section 11:

> During a period of some fifteen years covered by the Second World War and its immediate aftermath, homosexual offences of an indictable character increased between fourfold and fivefold ... In 1938 there were 134 cases of sodomy and bestiality known to the police in England and Wales. The number in 1952 was 670 ... Offences of gross indecency between males went up from 320 to 1,686. Importuning also increased substantially, 373 cases of proceedings in London alone being reported in 1952. In commenting on these figures in the House of Commons, the Under-Secretary for Home Affairs (Sir Hugh Lucas-Tooth) admitted he was baffled ...
>
> The reasons may not have been known to the minister, but to anyone such as the present writer who has studied the matter ... they are demonstrably attributable, at least in great part, to an excess of zeal on the part of the police ... it was easier and incidentally safer and less troublesome for a police officer to catch a homosexual than a burglar ... The drive against homosexuals proceeded on a relatively minor scale until 1951, when it suddenly began to be intensified as the result of ... the flight of the two British diplomats Guy Burgess and Donald Maclean in March 1951 and their defection to the Soviet Union. Both men were homosexuals ...
>
> In Britain the campaign reached its height in the latter part of 1953 and the early months of 1954, receiving a big fillip from the appointment as Metropolitan Police Commissioner of Sir John Nott-Bower, who, according to one report, 'swore he would rip the cover off all London's filth spots' ... The new Metropolitan Police Commissioner was

a man after the Home Secretary's heart, and together with Sir Theobald Mathew, who still held the office of Director of Public Prosecutions, they set the stage for the full-scale harrying of male homosexuals which was to take place during the succeeding months. Sir David Maxwell-Fyfe [the Home Secretary] made it clear that they must expect no mercy.[7]

Alan Turing was not alone at the centre of this maelstrom. More famous personages (in their day) than he found themselves in the dock: the writer Rupert Croft-Cooke; Lord Montagu of Beaulieu, tried as a trio with Michael Pitt-Rivers and Peter Wildeblood in March 1954 in a blaze of press attention; the actor Sir John Gielgud, convicted in 1953 of 'persistently importuning for immoral purposes'. Croft-Cooke had been warned that the police were 'always on the look-out for a well-publicised conviction'. Justice could not be done to any of these people, famous or otherwise, by pardoning Alan Turing.

In addition to the unfairness of singling out Alan Turing, simply because by 2012 people had heard of him, the notion of a 'pardon' is itself absurd. If you have offended me in some way, it is a gracious and noble thing for me to pardon you; this is the role of the Crown when offenders can, for good reasons, be excused. Many people resent the inference that Alan Turing had 'offended' in any way which merited a pardon, and I suspect he felt that way himself. If anything, it is Alan Turing who should be graciously pardoning the Crown for what was done in its name, not the other way round. Furthermore, there is something nonsensically anachronistic about it. In 1952 he was guilty, as the law stood, and there was nothing special about Alan Turing or the facts of his case which meant that he should be given a pardon. A logic which allows Alan Turing to be pardoned means that every person ever convicted under an old criminal statute which has been repealed should be pardoned. Finally, I don't see what was wrong with the apology: surely that made the point, convincingly and in a way which acknowledged the plight of others, using Alan's name as a vehicle to apologise to a whole community for an official system whose values were – however they seemed at the time – simply wrong.

On the other hand, many people saw the royal pardon issued by the queen (at the behest of her government – outside the UK it is not widely understood that she has no personal decision on these matters) on 24 December 2013 to Alan Turing as a tremendous symbol, with Alan's name standing proxy for all the others treated so dismally in the anti-gay crackdowns of the early 1950s and after. To that extent I can support it, but the mixture of feelings was too complicated for me to feel able to comment on the pardon at the time.

Since then, there have been further changes of government, and in early 2017 a new piece of legislation which has become known as 'Alan Turing's law' made it onto the statute book. This is supposed to right the wrong of singling out Alan Turing for a pardon and to confer pardons on everyone in his position. Surely there can be nothing but praise for such a thing? Unfortunately, it's not so simple, and the difficulties are buried in the convolutions of the new statute. Take a deep breath and follow me along this tortuous path.

Section 164(1) of the Policing and Crime Act 2017 automatically pardons, without any ado or process or fuss, a person who has been convicted of, or cautioned for, an offence on a list set out in subsection (3). The offences are a variety of sexual offences, including even a statute from the time of Henry VIII, but most relevantly our old favourite Section 11 of the Criminal Law Amendment Act 1885. What could be wrong with any of that? Only the fact that the automatic pardons apply if the person in question 'has died before this section comes into force'.

So if you're dead, you're pardoned; what if you're actually alive?

Section 165 is the section dealing with live people. In this case, the list of offences is shorter (but it does include Section 11 of the 1885 Act), and it applies if the person's conviction or caution has become 'disregarded' under the Protection of Freedoms Act 2012.

Just to explain: 'disregard' is a rather clumsy word which avoids the awkward connotations of a 'pardon' being given in the wrong direction. A conviction or caution which is disregarded means that details of the conviction or caution are to be deleted from official records, and the person 'is to be treated for all purposes in law as if the person has not committed the offence'.

To get a conviction or caution 'disregarded' under the 2012 Act it is necessary to apply to the Secretary of State, and it will only be granted if three things are established: (1) the other person involved in the conduct constituting the offence consented; (2) the other person was aged 16 or over; and (3) it was not a case of sexual activity in a public lavatory. Then it is up to the Secretary of State. An oral hearing is not allowed.[8]

Let's look at how this piece of liberalism works out in practice. For a live person to get a pardon, they have to prove the almost impossible, unless their co-defendant is somehow able to help with the evidence. In cases where people pleaded guilty there will be no court records which establish consent, though the age and the involvement of a public loo will probably be on the record. According to a Freedom of Information request I made, in the three years 2017–19, 182 applications were made covering 298 convictions or cautions. Of these, 78 convictions and cautions were disregarded – just over a quarter of them.

It seems that the majority of rejections are because the offence was outside the scope of the short list in Section 165.

It is hardly the great erasure of past shame which you might imagine from the politically catchy phrase 'Alan Turing's law'. To my mind, the shame is perpetuated in that we treat the dead better than the living, and pretend to have done justice where all we have been able to do is devise a complex and demeaning procedure which puts people through their old nightmare a second time around. Unfortunately, it's one more case of the narrative having overtaken the truth. Distortion appears to be an occupational hazard where the story of the 'Nation's Icon of the Twentieth Century' is concerned.

ICON

In the last years of his life, Alan Turing was engaged on a completely new direction of research. It was the most pictorial – the most iconic – work of his life, and despite the prominence of his published paper on it in Google Scholar, the least well known to the public.

Alan had been vaguely interested in the growth and form of living things since childhood, but when he began attending meetings of the 'Ratio Club' in about 1950 the interest was rekindled. The Ratio Club was an informal grouping of non-professors (in Britain only the chief of an academic department is a 'professor', and the senior, but non-professor, academics of the Ratio Club wanted to be liberated from the conventionalities of their bosses) which met to discuss the emerging science of cybernetics. In 1950, this had nothing to do with information security but was about perception and control. Consider a robot exploring its environment: in order to appreciate that it is going to run into a wall, it needs to perceive the wall, and send signals to its motor functions to stop or change course. The control mechanisms to connect perception and response are the cybernetics. (Like 'robot', and without planning permission, 'cyber' is a word which has changed its use since the 1950s. Robots have become synonymous with AI and cyber with computer communications, leaving robotics and cybernetics in a kind of no man's land occupied only by, well, science-fiction movies.)

Control systems for robots were about programming, which is where Alan Turing originally came in. Control also went beyond robots. The non-professors included a high-energy school of biologists, who were trying to answer similar questions about how animals avoid walking into walls. The biologists were also interested in morphogenesis, the development of shape and pattern in early life. This subject overlapped with mathematics in interesting ways – not least that Alan Turing's professor, M.H.A. Newman, had written the textbook on topology (stretchy geometry). In 1950, while the barometer measuring whether computers can think was forecasting a moderate gale, Alan started to conjecture that the behaviour of chemicals in a developing animal or plant might be modelled mathematically, and that the model might give answers to some of the mysterious questions about how asymmetry develops in living organisms. It isn't obvious how a completely spherical ball of cells can begin the process of differentiation and specialisation. To upset the symmetry, something needs to disturb it, and that something must come from inside the perfectly symmetrical object.

Alan Turing's work on how this might happen was presented to the Ratio Club on 8 February 1952, just before the storm of the 'gross indecency' arrest and trial broke. His paper 'The Chemical Basis of Morphogenesis' was published in the Proceedings of the Royal Society in the same year. Written before the self-replicating structure of DNA was discovered, it was a major breakthrough in developmental biology. Unlike

Alan's work on mathematical logic, cryptanalysis or computer programming, this is colourful, three-dimensional, and illustrated by his own drawings of what is going on.[1]

Florets – which will develop into seeds – in a sunflower head have a special symmetry in that they are aligned in spirals going both clockwise and anticlockwise, with the number of spirals being in the Fibonacci series (0, 1, 1, 2, 3, 5, 8, 13 … where the next number is made by adding the two preceding ones). You can see the same phenomenon on a stalk of brussels sprouts which are often on sale at Christmastime, though counting the spirals on sprouts is not easy. Alan's work, at the time of his death, was focused on modelling these patterns, understanding the balance of chemical influences as the stalk grows and the plant 'decides' where the next sprout is going to sprout.

For some reason, this work is still scarcely known and barely registers with the public. Maybe that's because his theory was wrong? It seems not, since in 2014, American researchers demonstrated that chemicals can indeed diffuse in the way he modelled.[2] Another possibility is that, because the new direction Alan's research was taking happened to coincide with his trial and the unavoidable publicity of his sexuality, it was dismissed by the scientific community. Either they didn't want to

A stalk of spiralling sprouts.

talk about him, or (which is the same thing) they didn't want to talk about his theory. In other words, was he straight-washed out of the picture? This might have some traction, since Alan himself wrote to his friend Norman Routledge shortly after his broadcast debate with Professors Braithwaite, Newman and Jefferson on whether machines could think:

> I'm rather afraid that the following syllogism may be used by some in the future
>> Turing believes machines think
>> Turing lies with men
>> Therefore machines do not think
> Yours in distress, Alan.[3]

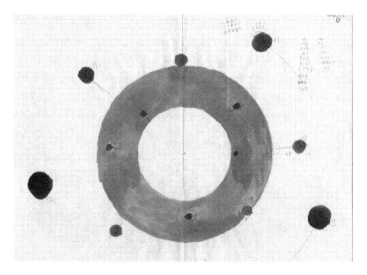

Buds emerging at a growth tip, as drawn by Alan Turing. (Reproduced by kind permission of the Provost and Scholars of King's College, Cambridge)

Of course he was in distress: the letter was written before the trial, which ended with a good legal outcome for someone who pleaded guilty – the things Alan feared did not come to be, and at the time he was writing, the sorcery called 'treatment by or under the direction of a duly qualified medical practitioner' was an unimagined future. Once the trial was over, the academic community (as contrasted with the *Third Programme* audience, possibly) didn't care what Alan's sexual preferences were. Insofar as they knew at all – which mainly they didn't since the media coverage of Alan's trial had been local only – it was part of the persona of someone who had awful trousers and a stammer and didn't wear a hat. Alan's postbag, as discovered in the Manchester filing cabinet, includes at least four requests for him to come and talk about his morphogenetic theory and a handful of offprint requests after his paper was published in late 1952.[4] I don't think the chemical theory of morphogenesis was ignored by developmental biologists because Alan Turing was gay. It may be that biologists have, or once had, an aversion to mathematical approaches, but there is probably a simpler explanation.

Rather, it seems that developmental biology is the province of other heroes, namely Francis Crick and Jim Watson, whose names are indelibly associated with the discovery of the double-helix structure of DNA – their paper being published in April 1953. Crick and Watson are the icons of developmental biology: they were awarded (together with Maurice Wilkins) a Nobel Prize in 1962, and Francis Crick has a research institute named after him in London, which is happily situated next-door to the British Library which houses the Alan Turing Institute, the 'national institute for data science and artificial intelligence'. No matter that the actual science – the X-ray crystallography that revealed the helical structure – was done by Rosalind Franklin in Wilkins's lab, even if Crick and Watson did the jigsaw-puzzle work with the complementing base pairs. She didn't get a look-in on the Nobel award, and somehow found herself airbrushed out of the story. Without her work, nobody would have heard of Francis Crick. It wasn't exactly intellectual theft, but it was a case of wilful oversight, of sexism in action, for Rosalind Franklin was a woman, and because she died in 1958 she wasn't around to complain.

Alan Turing's place in the pantheon is different: his role is to be the icon of Bletchley Park. He would be the first to admit that the codebreakers were a team; he felt that being one of a handful of senior personnel given an OBE for the work done there was a piece of nonsense. (He kept the medal in his tool-box.) It's not quite the whitewash, or perhaps malewash, story of DNA, because the present-day museum at Bletchley Park tries its hardest to explain the roles of other, greater, code-breakers like Dilly Knox, John Tiltman and Bill Tutte, and to tell the stories of the women at Bletchley. But popular appetite demands an exhibition on Alan Turing, because he is the symbol of the place.

Symbology and iconography take the place of real history: the standard, glib picture of 'War Hero Alan Turing, Persecuted and Died for his Sexuality' is almost religious in its narrative. He was named by BBC2 viewers as the 'nation's icon', the 'greatest person of the 20th century', beating Pablo Picasso, Muhammad Ali, David Bowie, Ernest Shackleton and Nelson Mandela in a bizarre election run-off which took place in February 2019. The BBC's website celebrates the victory with a quote: 'Those who can imagine anything, can create the impossible.'

The *Oxford Dictionary of English Etymology* tells me that the word 'icon' means an image, a picture, and in the Eastern Church, a 'representation in the flat of a sacred personage', and that it derives from the Greek word *eikon*. The 1864 edition of Liddell and Scott's Greek–English lexicon (as close as I can get to Ancient Greek) gives εἰκών (eikon) as 'a figure, image, likeness. II. a semblance, phantom, wraith', which implies that what you see in an icon is not what you get. Indeed. Although Alan Turing has become, in a sense, a sacred personage, the icon is only the 'representation in the flat' of the real person. The standard narrative is too flattened to be true, just like the fake quote on the BBC website, which I cannot find anywhere in Alan Turing's published papers or his speeches.

If you search the Internet for 'Alan Turing Quotations' you will find a number of websites which list his most popular quotes. One site which does this garners the most 'likes' (560) for: 'Sometimes it is the people no one can imagine anything of who do the things no one can imagine.' Most of the other thirty-six quotes are accompanied with source data so you can check for yourself where they come from. If we ignore those that are in Finnish, Spanish and Italian – although these, being in languages not spoken by Alan Turing, may be suspect, most seem to be translations of the English quotes – we've still got a handful of strange quotes which I don't recognise as coming from his pen. Some can, in fact, be traced to a different source: the script for the film *The Imitation Game*. In the movie, the words of the top-scoring quote – 'Sometimes it is the very people who no one imagines anything of who do the things that no one can imagine' – were spoken not only by the Alan Turing character but also by Christopher Morcom and Joan Clarke. Never mind; you can buy an inspirational Alan Turing Quote Plaque to hang in your office, engraved with these words and attributed to the icon himself, from Amazon.

The fake quote on the BBC website, 'Those who can imagine anything can create the impossible', looks similar, but is a tougher nut to crack. Dozens of businesses and schools have adopted this aphorism as an inspirational strapline, so it's too late to disavow the quote, even though Alan Turing never said it, and neither did the scriptwriter for *The Imitation Game*. Some commentators suggest that Jules Verne said it (but if so, he said it in French, and even then the actual source is questionable). Web pages posted to Google only seem to have begun attributing the phrase to Alan Turing in about 2016; it's remarkable that he could utter new quotable quotes some sixty years after his death, but maybe this is what one should expect of a sacred personage.

As well as being a fertile source of now-indelible fake quotes, the film has become the definitive representation in the flat of the sacred personage we now know as Alan Turing. In the film, the character of Alan Turing speaks certain words, so they become Alan Turing's words, and in the same way the character written in the script and played by Benedict Cumberbatch becomes Alan Turing himself. The script's portrait of Alan as socially dysfunctional is unfair, his career was not shaped by the attack on Enigma, and the standard narrative of Alan's suicide being attributable to the cruelty of the state is blown out of all proportion; but these things are now fixed in the public mind as being what define Alan Turing's character, work and life.

I am often asked what I make of *The Imitation Game* – it probably tops the list of popular questions. In fact, it's a great movie with plenty of plot twists and interesting characters, and taken on that level it deserved the one Oscar that it won. Sometimes, though, people are wary of the Hollywood approach and want to know which bits of the movie are right, and which are not. To list all the departures from the 'truth' and all the liberties taken with time, place, character and so forth would be tedious; only a moment's thought is enough to remind one that a feature film and a documentary are different things. This is so even when the feature film is a biopic, based on a true story, the dramatisation of a serious historical work. Still, the *New York Review of Books* was pretty scathing:

> In [the film] version of events, Turing and his small group of fellow codebreakers spend the first two years of the war in fruitless isolation; only in 1941 does Turing's crazy machine finally show any results ... What this account neglects to mention is that Turing's 'bombes' – electromechanical calculating devices designed to reconstruct the settings of the Enigma – were already helping to decipher German army and air force codes from early on ...
>
> The filmmakers see their hero above all as a martyr of a homophobic Establishment, and they are determined to lay emphasis on his victimhood. *The Imitation Game* ends with the following title: 'After a year of government-mandated hormonal therapy, Alan Turing committed suicide in 1954.' This is in itself something of a distortion ... the whole miserable episode ended in 1953 – a full year before his death, something not made clear to the filmgoer.[5]

The critic concludes that the whole thing is 'monstrous hogwash' and that, 'In perhaps the most bitter irony of all, the filmmakers have managed to transform the real Turing, vivacious and forceful, into just the sort of mythological gay man, whiney and weak, that homophobes love to hate'.

In short, *The Imitation Game* may be a great movie but it is second-rate history. Whether you think that a film which is 'based on the incredible true story' (according to the poster) ought to stick more closely to historical fact depends on what you think movies are for. What can be said without controversy is that this particular film stimulated interest among a wider public in the life of Alan Turing, and more importantly, in the work of Bletchley Park. The upswing in visitor numbers (until the horrible intervention of Coronavirus) there helped the museum to escape dependency on handouts for its existence and to improve and broaden the stories which it, with painstaking verification of accuracy, seeks to tell. Meanwhile, we are supposed to be intelligent enough to be able to distinguish between news and fake news, or even between a museum and an evening's entertainment.

Yet I wonder how much of what we see in films insinuates itself as the truth. First impressions are important, and when script and actors combine to tell a powerful story, the details somehow become real. I am asked very odd questions about Alan Turing from time to time – here's one: 'Why did Alan Turing put secret coded messages in his socks?' – and have to remind myself that, unwittingly, people have remembered scenes from a film, which have become brushstrokes in some kind of portrait.

Artworks, novels and musical works are different. Artists are usually trying to tell you something new about their subject, to make you change your perception. Books, by contrast, are more troublesome. There is no quality kitemark which tells you whether a biography of Alan Turing (I am aware of at least a dozen) is any good. What do I mean by that? I suppose a biography ought to be an unbiased description and assessment from what is found in the evidence, but the majority of those on my list are digests or rehashes of the very small number of biographies which were actually based on examination of primary resources: documents, interviews and contemporary commentary. No doubt these secondary writers add their own layer of interpretation and discussion, but there must be some

One of Justin Eagleton's Turing series, celebrating Manchester Pride.
(Reproduced by kind permission of Justin Eagleton)

question as to the validity of conclusions reached through interpreting someone else's interpretation. Novels, like artworks, aim to expose truths or deeper thinking by approaching their subject sideways; they may intrigue and draw the reader into fantasy, but there is no deception in their approach. Somewhere in between the novel and the pseudo-biography is a bizarre graphical bio-book about Alan Turing, in which Christopher Morcom makes an appearance as a bee – perhaps enough said.

What makes us turn a person into an icon, a sacred personage, seems to be a question of fashion. While I am writing this, there is a national debate in progress about the statuary which graces, or clutters, our town centres and imposing buildings. Statues appear to commemorate people who were not always first rate or particularly memorable, even in their own day, and whose values clash with our own. One wonders what the fate of Alan Turing's statues will be, in a century or two; no matter, as many of them have remarkably little resemblance to him anyway. He would no doubt have remembered that statues were banned in Erewhon.

It is perhaps instructive to remember that Alan Turing came twenty-first, not first, in the 2002 BBC series to find the 'Greatest Briton', again using the specious device of a television poll. First, in 2002, was Winston Churchill, with Isambard Kingdom Brunel and Princess Diana in the silver and bronze places. Diana had been dead only five years, and I observe that the tree in my local park which was planted to commemorate her has discreetly lost its explanatory label during the last twenty years. Her Majesty the Queen came twenty-fourth in 2002, three places behind Alan. I don't know what any of this means, except that our choices (or rather, the choices of those who participate in BBC polls) wax and wane, and that we seem to like slightly flawed characters who died young. (In the top ten 'Greatest Britons' were John Lennon (8) and Lord Nelson (9) who, like Diana and Alan, died before they reached their 50th birthday.)

Choosing a figure to put on the new plastic £50 note cannot have been easy for the Bank of England. The erstwhile Governor, Mark Carney, explained the process in a letter to an MP:[6]

> In 2013, a new process for choosing characters was put in place that invited public nominations but also set up the Banknote Character Advisory Committee, with significant independent representation, to help choose the nomination field and to shortlist characters. For the £50 note, they chose the field of 'science' in recognition of the United Kingdom's extraordinary scientific heritage. For the £50 note, as for the £20 note, we also held a public nomination process for eligible characters in the chosen field. This helps to ensure we are considering as broad a range of potential candidates as possible, and listening to who the UK public would like to see represented on their banknotes. We have been delighted by the enthusiastic response of the public to the character selection process. Over the 6 week nomination period we received 227,299 nominations covering 989 eligible scientists.

That clearly doesn't make the process easy. The committee produced a shortlist of 'twelve' British scientists (two of whom were double-acts). Five of the fourteen names were women, including Rosalind Franklin; only one, the mathematician Srinivasa Ramanujan, was not ethnically white (and in any case, I thought he was Indian); only one was disabled (the structure-of-the-universe physicist Stephen Hawking); and

I wonder if that Alan Turing was not the only gay man on the list, not that it matters hugely what the sexuality of the nominees may have been. It wouldn't have been possible, I suspect, to tick all diversity boxes when choosing just one name.

Having chosen Alan, congratulations are due to the Bank of England for choosing a correctly attributed quote for the note. The chosen phrase, 'This is only a foretaste of what is to come, and only the shadow of what is going to be,' doesn't appear in any paper or publication by Alan either; but at least we have a contemporary record of his having said it, in the form of that old *Times* newspaper report from June 1949. One might sniff at the image on the note of the Pilot ACE computer (a machine disavowed by Alan), no doubt because the actual computers Alan worked on were not as photogenic; and – a much worse sin – at the portrait of Alan showing him with brushed hair and

a neatly tied tie, something only experienced on formal occasions (in this case his official photograph on becoming a Fellow of the Royal Society). Not that we could have someone untidy gracing our highest-denomination banknote, someone who is, after all, Britain's iconic scientist.

Various committee members explained their choice of Alan in a short video clip issued by the Bank of England. It's clear that the powerful standard narrative that the hormone treatment meted out to Alan 'led' to his suicide has been in their minds, and one of them said that 'Alan Turing's legacy, is without a doubt, up to 20 million lives that he saved during the Second World War'. Forgive me if I am a doubter, but I prefer the rationale of committee member Dr Maggie Aderin-Pocock – 'his work covered so much'.

The question of 'Alan Turing's legacy' is one I am often asked at the end of a talk about Alan Turing. This might be considered an odd question, given that I have usually spent the last forty minutes or so describing his work and its impact in the present – clearly that's not what the question means. I suspect it's about icons and what Alan ought to symbolise, and how we can – as with other sacred personages – be directed in our own lives by his example. My suspicion is that people want to be reassured that the work of Bletchley Park really was something that transformed the war, and that it gives us permission to think about the war as something clean and intellectual, that the Allied victory was achieved clinically by the application of brains rather than bombs. We can sweep Hamburg and Dresden aside and ignore the 36,000 German servicemen and 36,000 Allied merchant fleet sailors who died in the U-boat war if we read a 'Ladybird book' version of history which tells us that the conflict was put to an end by the heroic boffinry of a single man. And then we want to know that the inhumane treatment which Alan Turing was made to endure is something we have moved on from, so that we can feel positive about our own lives and the world we have voted into existence.

I disagree with all of that, of course. Alan Turing does have a legacy, but it's a different one. His achievements, rather than his symbolism, are what we should remember: that astonishing list of things, 'On Computable Numbers' to 'The Chemical Basis of Morphogenesis', via 'Computing Machinery and Intelligence'. These things can inspire; and thinking about him, and where he came from and where he went to, can help us improve the rather unsatisfactory world we have indeed voted into existence. To quote the (actual) final sentence of 'Computing Machinery and Intelligence': 'We can only see a short distance ahead, but we can see plenty there that needs to be done.' Here is the basis for an agenda:

- The Association of Computing Machinery instituted the 'A.M. Turing Award' in 1966. This is considered to be the equivalent of a Nobel Prize in the field of computer science. In the first fifty years the Award was won twice by a woman; the first woman to win it was Fran Allen in 2006. Women were the computer science pioneers – women like Beatrice Worsley and Cicely Popplewell, who mastered the complexities of backwards-hexadecimal coding. There is no shortage of female role models in computing – yet it's perceived to be a man's world. (There is also no shortage of female role models in X-ray work, either; in addition to Rosalind Franklin, another nominee for the £50 note was the crystallographer Dorothy Hodgkin. Edith and Florence Stoney didn't make the cut, but it would be greedy to expect more nominees to be women X-ray pioneers or related to me in some way.) Partly this is because men write the histories, and men like machines, and so they write about the men that designed and built the machines. And partly it's because in the dark days of post-war social reaction women were gradually eased out of cutting-edge jobs in computing and sent back to domestic tasks. 'Starting when computer technology first emerged during World War Two and continuing into the 1960s, women made up most of the computing workforce. By 1970, however, women only accounted for 13.6% of bachelor's in computer science graduates. In 1984 that number rose to 37%, but it has since declined to 18%.'[7] Those are American statistics, but it would be absurd to suggest that this is just an American problem. It is modern society and cultural attitudes, and exclusion of women from iconic recognition through Nobel Prizes and ACM Awards, that discourage girls from choosing science and technology subjects for senior-level study and careers.

- If the under-representation of women in computer science is bad enough, people from black, Asian and minority ethnic groups face additional challenges. In 2014, a report highlighted that black and minority ethnic men were 28 per cent less likely to work in STEM than white men, and it's not clear that things have improved much since then.[8] According to the charity BBSTEM, only 6.2 per cent of UK domiciled students enrolled in STEM subjects at UK universities are black; 2011 census data for England and Wales have BAME (including mixed ethnicity) people at 13.7 per cent of the population. Talking about the problem may help: for example, in arts and social sciences, students and their lecturers tend to talk about sociological issues and this raises awareness; in science and maths, the academic focus is on the technical side, so 'STEM students and even academic staff tend to be less clued up on the realities of racism and how it affects their BAME peers at university.'[9] The Empire dies only slowly: sometimes things seem not to have changed much since John Turing was excluded from 'John Company' in 1791. If Alan Turing had been Indian by ethnicity or female by gender, it's not at all obvious that he would have been able to indulge his passion for science and mathematics, and to go on to found computer science.

- The fake news idea that 'Alan Turing's law' has somehow made it all right for gay people past and present so we can now move on needs to be challenged. In a belt of seventy-two countries across Africa, the Middle East and South-east Asia, around half of which are 'Commonwealth' countries, gay people can still be treated as criminals for their sexual preference.[10] Even where it's not criminal, it may be perfectly legal to discriminate against someone, there may be a danger of blackmail, and (even in Europe) homosexuality can be regarded officially as a type of infectious mental disease needing treatment. Attacks on human rights legislation are not going to help combat these medieval attitudes.

- Fake news is spread virally through social media. I'm not so sure that Alan Turing would have found social media an unconditional delight – even in 1954, he hadn't had a telephone connected to his house in Wilmslow. It is a paradox that what enables freedom of information and exchange of ideas actually strengthens and reinforces dotty, and in some cases harmful, stories which have no basis in evidence. Another paradox is that GCHQ, the successor to Bletchley Park which was the home of the hackers, is now a champion of communications security through its offshoot the National Cyber Security Centre (which has nothing to do with robots, at least not the scrap-iron-eating kind). Despite our concerns for security and privacy, we share nonsense on social media, and scatter data about our preferences through our Internet searches and purchases and through the Internet of things, allowing vast databanks to be created which insidiously manipulate our choices – and not just our buying choices – in unseen ways. We do not control this or understand it any better than we control AI, and if we ignore the peril we will receive the governments we deserve.

- Bias creeps into AI not only through reinforcing our prejudices and buying preferences. Machines learn what we want, and commercial drivers ensure that those with the most disposable cash are enthusiastically preferred as customers. Bias in AI, driven by reinforcement learning algorithms, is not just about silly photo-identification bots in phones being unable to correctly identify a black person as such because it was trained on a data-set of white faces. All recognition systems – so, essentially, all machine learning – involves discrimination: deciding which side of a line something falls on. Not all discrimination is bad, but it needs to be overseen to ensure that it is fair. We should stop visualising the dangers of AI in terms of road accidents involving self-driving cars, and vet the AI producers for unfair discrimination, as well as for the value systems which direct the development of more advanced AI systems.

So, here is my suggestion. I'd like to ask for 'No more fake quotes', but let's be realistic:

1. **No more John William Turings or Ethel Stoneys.** Enable kids from BAME groups to thrive in STEM subjects, and change our social attitude so we allow more girls to find a career in tech.
2. **No more sniggering about robots.** Regulate AI research intelligently, and impose 'MOT'-type tests on all sorts of AI systems, not just self-driving cars.
3. **No more Alan Turing's laws.** Instead, put pressure on Commonwealth and other nations to remove anti-gay laws and practices.

In the Bank of England video, Dr Simon Singh said, 'When we look at the fifty pound note, and we look at Alan Turing, I hope we think about the amazing things that humans can do, and the amazing contributions to science that Britain has made, but I also hope we think about the way we want the world to be in the future, and how we should all treat each other.' Surely that is what his legacy should be.

NOTES

RAJ

1   For the history of the Turings in Madras, see Henry Davison Love, *Vestiges of Old Madras* (John Murray, 1913).
2   On William Turing and John William Turing, see India Office Records, British Library: IOR/L/AG/34/29/186, IOR/B/113.
3   Quoted in Love, op. cit., vol. III, p.179.
4   William Dalrymple, *White Mughals: Love and Betrayal in Eighteenth Century India* (Harper Press, 2012) p. xlviii.
5   Walter Del Mar, *India of To-Day* (Adam and Charles Black, 1905).
6   This and other quotations from John Turing's unpublished autobiography, *The Half was not Told Me* (1980).
7   E.W. Stoney's account in the *Minutes of the Proceedings of the Institution of Civil Engineers*, vol. CCII, pp.50–2 (1917).
8   *Ibid.* Vol. CIII, Pt 1, pp.135–50 (1891).

X-RAY

1   Sara Turing, *Alan M. Turing* (W. Heffer & Sons, 1959).
2   For G.J. Stoney and his daughters, see Adrian Thomas and Francis Duck, *Edith and Florence Stoney, Sisters in Radiology* (Springer Biographies, 2019).

3　Rita McWilliams-Tullberg, *Women at Cambridge* (Victor Gollancz, 1975).

4　Eleanor Ireland, quoted in Jack Copeland (ed.), *Colossus* (Oxford University Press, 2006), p.161.

5　Janet Abbate, *Inventing the Internet* (MIT Press, 1999); Marie Hicks, *Programmed Inequality* (MIT Press, 2017).

6　'Turned Away at the Gates', varsity.co.uk/features/17317 (2019).

7　*How can we increase girls' uptake of maths and physics A-level?* Cassidy, Cattan, Crawford and Dytham: Report for the IFS (August 2018).

8　Mihaela van der Schaar, Turing Institute blog (February 2020).

9　US District Court Colorado, Case 1:20-cv-00152-LTB, Verified Complaint for Forfeiture in Rem.

COMPUTE

1　See Juliet Floyd and Alisa Bokulich (eds), *Philosophical Explorations of the Legacy of Alan Turing* (Springer, 2017), especially Chapter 5.

2　Andrew Hodges, *Alan Turing: The Enigma* (Burnett Books, 1983).

3　'On Computable Numbers, with an application to the Entscheidungsproblem', *Proceedings of the London Mathematical Society*, series 2, vol. 42, pp.230–65 (1936).

4　*Proceedings of the London Mathematical Society*, series 2, vol. 45, pp. 161–228 (1938).

5　B.V. Bowden (ed.), *Faster than Thought* (Pitman, 1953).

6　University of Manchester Archive, TUR/ADD/43.

7　*Electronics* magazine (September 1951, p.81).

8　King's College Archive, AMT/B/6.

9　King's College Archive, AMT/A/13.

10　Andrew Hodges, op. cit., p.477.

11　King's College Archive, AMT/K/1/79.

12　See Andrew Hodges's website: www.turing.org.uk.

13　'Some Calculations of the Riemann Zeta-function', *Proceedings of the London Mathematical Society*, Series 3, vol. 3, pp.99–117 (1952).

GEHEIM

1   J.H. Wilkinson, *Some comments from a numerical analyst* (1970 ACM Turing Award lecture).
2   See 'Alan Turing: The codebreaker who saved "millions of lives"' www.bbc.co.uk/news/technology-18419691.
3   Cambridge University Security Group seminar, 19 October 1993; see also 'British Intelligence in the Second World War: An Overview', *Cryptologia*, vol. 14(1), pp.1–10 (1990).
4   David Kenyon, *Bletchley Park and D-Day* (Yale University Press, 2019), pp.252–3.
5   See Dermot Turing, *Codebreakers of Bletchley Park* (Arcturus, 2020), p.62.
6   The National Archives, Reference HW 14/2.
7   'The Turing Bombe: Was it Enough?', *Cryptologia*, vol. 14(4), pp.331–49.
8   A.P. Mahon, *History of Hut 8*, reproduced in B. Jack Copeland (ed.), *The Essential Turing* (Oxford University Press, 2004).
9   I.J. Good in F.H. Hinsley and Alan Stripp (eds), *Codebreakers: The Inside Story of Bletchley Park* (Oxford University Press, 1993), p.155.
10 Dermot Turing, *The Bombe Breakthrough* (Bletchley Park, 2018), p.83.
11 This and subsequent quotations from his unpublished autobiography, *The Half was not Told Me* (1980).
12 Geoffrey Pidgeon, *The Secret Wireless War* (UPSO, 2006), Chapters 18, 29.
13 Geek's Guide, *The Register*, 5 July 2013.
14 Andrew Hodges, op. cit., p.290.

ROBOT

1   See B. Jack Copeland (ed.), *Alan Turing's Automatic Computing Engine* (Oxford University Press, 2005), pp.40, 77, 104, 369.
2   *Daily Telegraph*, 7 November 1946.
3   Reproduced in Copeland, *The Essential Turing*.
4   See www.alanturing.net, Darwin to Appleton, 23 July 1947.

5 *Intelligent Machinery* (1948), reproduced in Copeland, *The Essential Turing*.

6 Mike Woodger, reported in Bernard Meltzer and Donald Michie (eds), *Machine Intelligence 5* (Edinburgh University Press, 1969), p.3.

7 Science and Technology Committee, HC 145, 12 October 2016, para 7.

8 See Copeland, *The Essential Turing*, p.409.

9 1949 Lister Oration, *British Medical Journal*, 25 June 1949.

10 *The Times*, 11 June 1949.

11 *Daily Telegraph*, 31 January 1950.

12 *Mind*, vol. 59 (1950), pp.433–60.

13 Reproduced in Copeland, *The Essential Turing*.

14 John Searle, 'What Your Computer Can't Know', *New York Review of Books*, 9 October 2014.

15 Roger Penrose, *The Emperor's New Mind* (Oxford University Press, 1989), p.579.

16 King's College Archive, AMT/D/4.

17 'The Myth of AI', John Brockman: www.edge.org/conversation/jaron_lanier-the-myth-of-ai.

18 Manuel Alfonseca et al., *Superintelligence cannot be contained: Lessons from Computability Theory*, arXiv:1607.00913.

19 European Parliament Report with recommendations to the Commission on Civil Law Rules on Robotics (2015/2103(INL)).

20 Stuart Russell and Peter Norvig, *Artificial Intelligence: A Modern Approach* (4th Edition, Pearson, 2020), Chapter 27.

21 www.edge.org, e-conversation.

22 Viking, 2019, p.249.

23 'Can digital machines think?', Radio broadcast 15.5.51, reproduced in Copeland, *The Essential Turing*.

POSTBAG

1 *University of Manchester News*, 25 August 2017.

2 University of Manchester Archive, TUR/ADD/140.

3 University of Manchester Archive, TUR/ADD/28.

4 Jonathan Peter Bowen, 'The Impact of Alan Turing: Formal Methods and Beyond', in Jack Copeland et al. (eds), *The Turing Guide* (Oxford University Press, 2017); see also Scott M. Campbell,

'Beatrice Helen Worsley: Canada's Female Computer Pioneer', *IEEE Annals of the History of Computing*, vol. 25(4) (2003), pp.51–62.

5 All excerpts from University of Manchester Archive, TUR/ADD/91.

6 University of Manchester Archive, TUR/ADD/24, 48, 57, 59, 74, 88, 130.

7 University of Manchester Archive, TUR/ADD/64.

8 University of Manchester Archive, TUR/ADD/111.

9 Pages 313–14.

10 University of Manchester Archive, TUR/ADD/16, 33, 79.

11 Henry O'Connell and Michael Fitzgerald, *Irish Journal of Psychological Medicine*, vol. 201(1) (2003), pp.28–31.

12 This and following quotations of John Turing from 'My Brother Alan', in Sara Turing, *Alan M. Turing* (Centenary Edition, Cambridge University Press, 2012).

13 *Alan Turing: Colleagues share their memories*, BBC, 23 June 2012.

14 'Pioneering Work on Computers at Bletchley', in Nicholas Metropolis et al. (eds), *A History of Computing in the Twentieth Century* (Academic Press, 1980), p.34.

15 'Why code-breaker Alan Turing was cast aside by postwar Britain', *Mail Online*, 17 Nov. 2013.

16 King's College Archive, AMT/F/1.

17 King's College Archive, AMT/A/17/03. There may be errors in the revealed text as presented here.

18 Andrew Hodges, op. cit., p.496.

19 University of Manchester Archive, TUR/ADD/90.

20 University of Manchester Archive, TUR/ADD/92.

21 University of Manchester Archive, TUR/ADD/99, 100, 107.

22 University of Manchester Archive, TUR/ADD/35.

23 Quoted passages from this collection under reference AMT/D/4.

24 *Irish Times*, 14 September 2009.

APPLE

1 Mrs Clayton and inquest quotes taken from Andrew Hodges, *Alan Turing: The Enigma* (Centenary Edition, Vintage, 2012), pp.xxvii–xxviii, and King's College Archive, AMT/K/6.

2 US Department of Health Toxicological Profile for Cyanide (2006), p.42.
3 M.G. Gelder et al., *New Oxford Textbook of Psychiatry* (Oxford University Press, 2012); Janet Haines et al., 'The Characteristics of Those Who Do and Do Not Leave Suicide Notes', *OMEGA Journal of Death and Dying*, vol. 63(1) (2011), pp.79–94.
4 'My Brother Alan', in Sara Turing, [see Postbag note 12] op. cit.
5 'Interview with Rob Janoff, designer of the Apple logo', Creative Bits: www.creativebits.org/interview/interview_rob_janoff_ designer_apple_logo/.
6 See article in *Wired* by Stephen Levy, 14 Nov. 2014, and for the blog, blog.jgc.org/2009/06/alan-turing-deserves-apology-from.html.
7 *The Other Love* (William Heinemann, 1970), p.212.
8 See Protection of Freedoms Act 2012, sections 92, 94(2) and 96.

ICON

1 King's College Archive, AMT/K/3.
2 Nathan Tompkins et al., 'Testing Turing's theory of morphogenesis in chemical cells', *Proceedings of the National Academy of Sciences*, vol. 111(12) (2014), pp.4392–402.
3 King's College Archive, AMT/D/14a.
4 University of Manchester Archive, TUR/ADD/68, 84, 97, 121, 133, 134.
5 Christian Caryl writing on 19 November 2014.
6 15 February 2019, on Bank of England website: www. bankofengland.co.uk.
7 'The Current State of Women in Computer Science', *Computer Science*: www.computerscience.org/resources/women-in-computer-science/.
8 Campaign for Science and Engineering, *Improving Diversity in STEM* (May 2014).
9 Marianna Marcelline in *Glasgow Guardian*, 15 September 2019.
10 Human Dignity Trust: www.humandignitytrust.org/lgbt-the-law/map-of-criminalisation/.

FURTHER READING

There are innumerable books about Alan Turing and, indeed, about the various themes touched on in this book. Rather than provide a comprehensive bibliography, I have picked out a small selection of things which readers might find interesting or entertaining.

On the early days of the British Raj in India at the end of the eighteenth century, *White Mughals* by William Dalrymple (HarperPress, 2012) is a fascinating study of cross-cultural relationships interwoven with politics.

The careers of Florence and Edith Stoney are told in fuller detail by Adrian Thomas and Francis Duck in *Edith and Florence Stoney, Sisters in Radiology* (Springer Biographies, 2019). For a racier Stoney story, the tale of Andrew Robinson Stoney Bowes can hardly be beaten: see *Wedlock: How Georgian Britain's Worst Husband Met His Match* by Wendy Moore (Phoenix, 2009).

The Turing family history was put into terrible verse by the Rev. Henry Mackenzie, Vicar of St Martin-in-the-Fields, in 1849. His masterwork is called *The Lay of the Turings*, and mercifully its tiny print run means that few people will ever be exposed to its awfulness. Out of print for years, and having nothing to do with Turing family history, but a much better book all round is my father John Turing's *My Nephew Hamlet* (J.M. Dent & Sons, 1967). It's his best book, his only published foray into fiction and is an inside-out reworking of Shakespeare's play. Its only tenuous relevance to the story of Alan Turing is that John dedicated it to his brother – a posthumous attempt to heal an old wound. The dedication reads, 'To the memory of my brother Alan, whose genius, having another bent, was slow to concede merit in William Shakespeare's *magnum opus* save for the final stage direction.' To save you having to look it up, the direction is 'A dead march. Exeunt, bearing off the bodies; after which a peal of ordnance is shot off.' I think Alan would have enjoyed it. Get a second-hand copy if you can.

Less light-hearted but more suited to readers who want to delve further into Alan Turing's seminal paper *On Computable Numbers* is an annotated version by Charles Petzold called *The Annotated Turing* (Wiley Publishing, 2008), which takes the reader gradually through the entire text, explaining everything along the way. Another way to approach the paper is to look at its implications and influences, and there are several books of this type which also range around other aspects of Alan Turing's work. One that does not need two strong individuals to carry it to your armchair is *The Turing Guide*, edited by Jack Copeland, Jonathan Bowen, Mark Sprevak and Robin Wilson (Oxford University Press, 2017), the contributions in which were stimulated by the events, talks and thinking surrounding the centenary of Alan's birth in 2012.

Of the literally dozens of biographies of Alan Turing, unfortunately only a few can claim to be based on original research. My own *Prof: Alan Turing Decoded* (Pitkin, 2016) is one of these; beware those others which pick titbits selectively from the proper books and bury the facts beneath the writer's own narrative imagination. Hint: if there aren't any endnotes that refer to primary sources, it's quite possibly refried beans but rather less good for you.

The other people in Alan Turing's life should not be brushed out of history. I was commissioned to write *The Codebreakers of Bletchley Park* recently, because the stories of codebreakers other than Alan Turing are not as well known as they should be. In particular, there is a myth that the codebreakers were all men and the only jobs for women were menial ones; I hope that my new book (Arcturus Publishing, 2020) sets the record a bit straighter.

On the subject of women and degrees, Rita McWilliams-Tullberg wrote forcefully about it in *Women at Cambridge: A Men's University Though of a Mixed Type* in 1975. A newer edition of her book was issued in 1998 by the Cambridge University Press. On the post-war times there is an enjoyable book called *Alan Turing's Manchester* by Jonathan Swinton (Infang Publishing, 2019). Professor Swinton is one of the few academics who understands Alan Turing's unfinished work on plant morphogenesis, but this is a different book – approachable, fully illustrated and packed with interesting details about Manchester in the 1950s.

Finally, I should encourage anyone who has got this far to get a copy of Stuart Russell's *Human Compatible* (Viking, 2019). This explains why control of artificial intelligence is so important, and it's done by someone who not only knows what he is talking about but has the uncommon gift of making it simple for the lay reader.

INDEX

Note: *italicised* page references indicate illustrations.